THEIR WORDS
WERE
BULLETS

THEIR WORDS WERE BULLETS

*The Southern Press in War,
Reconstruction, and Peace*

HODDING CARTER

*MERCER UNIVERSITY LAMAR
MEMORIAL LECTURES, NO. 12*

UNIVERSITY OF GEORGIA PRESS

ATHENS

©

Contents

v

Foreword

WITH THE PUBLICATION OF THIS TWELFTH SERIES OF EUGENIA Dorothy Blount Lamar Memorial Lectures, delivered at Mercer University in February 1969, the Lamar Lecture Committee and the University reaffirm their gratitude to the late Mrs. Lamar's wisdom and generosity in endowing this perpetual series of lectures. Mrs. Lamar, a cultural leader in Macon and the the South for nearly three-quarters of a century, was keenly interested in the continuation of traditional Southern values amid the kaleidoscope of social and economic changes taking place in the modern South. She left a legacy to Mercer University with the request that it be used "to provide lectures of the very highest type of scholarship which will aid in the permanent preservation of the values of Southern culture, history, and literature."

Hodding Carter, who has carried on his lover's quarrel with the South amid great physical and psychic dangers, is a man of impressive presence. White-haired, barrel-chested, he reminded one of Hemingway as he stepped off the plane on a windswept February afternoon. A short ride from the airport was enough to establish Mr. Carter and his charming wife, Betty, as warm and witty conversationalists, urbane as well as humane. It was therefore with genuine regret that we came to realize that Mr. Carter was in the initial stages of a relapse of a bout with influenza. He was unable to deliver the lectures.

Fortunately, Mrs. Carter was able—on very short notice —to present her husband's lectures with a style and grace that led one Lamar committeeman to observe that hers was the "best platform performance in the eleven-year history of the series." Mrs. Carter, who had worked closely with her husband in the research for the writing of this history of journalism in the South, read the lectures with a great depth of understanding.

One hears and reads Hodding Carter's words with respect. He is one who has "been there" in the vanguard of Southern journalists who were attempting to interpret the South truthfully in a painful time of change. The elegant words of William Swain, a Greensboro publisher writing in the early 1830s, apply to Hodding Carter, who "would rather bask for one hour in the approving smiles of an intelligent and undeceived people, than to spend a whole eternity amidst the damning grins of a motley crew of office hunters, despots, demagogues, tyrants, fools, and hypocrites."

Benjamin W. Griffith, Jr., *Chairman*
The Lamar Lecture Committee

Mercer University
Macon, Georgia

Preface

THESE INTRODUCTORY COMMENTS ARE MADE DIFFICULT BE-
cause I am a Southern newspaperman myself, a student of
Southern history, and a person of prejudice and, I hope,
principle—all of which are bound to permeate these in-
trospective glances.

From my earliest years I have cherished three ambitions.
The primary one was to be a newspaper editor. The second was to own a hardware store. The third was to be a
restauranteur. It is probably no indifferent oddity that all
have had to do with smell: the dark smell of printer's ink,
the gleaming steely scent of hardware, the delicious blend-
ing odors of food.

I have managed to attain each of these sensory objectives. But as should be obvious the most difficult to obtain and most desirable has to do with printer's ink. And
when an amalgam of such ink and history is created, an
absorptive precipitation is the mental if not physical
result.

This little volume concerns one Southern amalgam,
the press, which for its disciples and devotees has scents
and sights and sounds of its own.

I am proud to be a Southern newspaperman. Despite
some shameful aberrations we live in a proud tradition.

I have carried a gun sometimes, in an olden manner, and twice I have used that gun, but without killing. I have stood with my elders and betters and dared the illdoers to do their worst. I have read and glorified in the defiant paeans of editors who are obscure save in the hushed lodges of their homelands.

This is America. I thank God that I have contributed something to its story.

HODDING CARTER

Greenville, Mississippi

ONE

Introduction

WHATEVER ELSE MAY BE SAID OF THE SOUTHERN PRESS, THE newspapers of the South have certainly demonstrated closer identification with the aspirations and turmoil and tragedy of their region than have those of any other part of the United States.

The Southern editors for 150 years have been spokesmen, defenders, and firebrands in their regions to an extent not in evidence anywhere except perhaps in the old West. They have used their type fonts as bullets, their newsprint as musket wadding, their ink as gunpowder, and their words as tinder.

To oversimplify the never simple is a temptation. But it can be said that the South's newspapers fall chronologically, as does its history, into four periods: the first was that of the embattled newspapers of the pre-Civil War period when the major issue had to do with the extension or abolition of slavery and the perpetuation or drastic modification of states' rights, and some of the press even said and believed that the South should go ahead and whip the insolent Northerners and so work out the answers through military power. This the newspapers and the politicians would find they could not do, if only because the South was lacking in the resources necessary to win a war and the manpower to match the overwhelming numbers of the North. The second period was that of the Civil War itself; the third that of Reconstruction, followed by the golden years of Henry Watterson and Henry Grady, who talked of peace and adaptation to the new order and who were great healers of wounds. This third period logically edges over into the fourth, that of the newspapers of our century when, unfortunately, there is an increasing lack of difference between a newspaper in Peoria and one in New Orleans. They buy the same columns, speak from the same vantage point, and rarely crusade. But in passing, and more than just in passing, let it be said here that an area that can claim the late Ralph McGill, Mark Ethridge, Hazel Brannon Smith, Harry Ashmore and his publisher Andrew Heiskell, Sylvan Myer —and these do not stand alone—need not apologize for its better newspapers, among which we may also include the Miami, Louisville, and Nashville newspapers, intermittently those of Richmond, and the valiant low-gauge press of North Carolina. There are others, of course.

What I am going to say about the newspapers of the South, historically and today, is predicated upon several assumptions. One is that the channels of communication in truly or partially free systems of government are greatly shaped by the events which they seek to report and reflect upon. A second is that the journalistic impact is something like a two-way street, for it helps to fashion and direct the eventual outcome of the events with which it deals. A third is that national conditions and national and international concerns help shape internal regional politics and the resultant upheavals have a cumulative and mammoth effect upon the press and the public which looks to it, with varying degrees of dependence, for guidance.

The impact of history and current events upon the free

and fettered press of the world is what makes the differences. There are today such cynical, frequently corrupt, newspapers as those of France, whose news and editorial columns have traditionally been purchasable, but which earlier gave much of the impetus for freedom. The once austere but radically changed British press has presently shaped—and not for good, in great part—today's American tabloid by seeking out the lowest common denominator in news reporting in a nation where once the majority of newspapers sought to emulate the integrity of the *Times* of London. But it stood for generations as a symbol of British stability, British incorruptibility, and—it must be said—British stodginess. Look further about us. The near savage femininity and endemic instability of the newspapers of Latin America—with a few courageous and brilliant exceptions—are simply expressions of Latin distaste for political order or true political good behavior and of a chronic failure to achieve or even seek for such orderliness. The twenty million dead for whose butchery Adolph Hitler was the authority and initiator might have been fewer by the millions had not the German press goose-stepped and dreamed of conquest by a triumphant fatherland while laying the blame for an earlier defeat upon everything but the German mentality and the German talent for making enemies and the German genius for making war and holding in contempt the less warlike.

The press of the South might have learned in time a lesson that is mostly yet unlearned. The Southern press, child of sectionalism and hate and fear begotten of bitterness, and defender of borders, which are defensible, and a morality, the slave morality, which is not, shows a sad reluctance to do so even today.

These comments may afford some insight into the workings of that press a century ago and now.

This is the story of that press, and perhaps an overly-affectionate interpretation of the whys that made it the tinder box when the cries for calm should have been sounded instead.

But first, something of the region in which a distinctly American press was born and nurtured and fell upon desolate times, without learning much at all except the virtue of a certain valor and the tenacity of printer's ink. In that tale a seeker can find genius and ignorance, the pain of the defeated and the implacability of the vengeful. And most clearly can we see the painful stamp of conformity on a one-time nation within a nation that needed conformity least of all.

These realities—for they were realities whatever else others may say today—must be comprehended at the beginning. This is one man's attempt to provide more comprehension of what other men have variously called madness and philosophical conflict and a supreme belief in the supremacy of a region and race.

This cannot be a detailed history of journalism in the United States or in the South. But perhaps a few historical glances may be worthwhile. It should be said that the means to satisfy the thirst for orderly information about current events existed in the American colonies a half century before the first colonial newspapers were published. The printers knew the consequences of offending the government. So, when the colonial journals did appear, most of them were published with a marked indifference to time and place, thanks principally to primitive means of news dissemination. They were highly personal for the most part and often clandestine. Historically, the first such publication in the colonies was the newspaper published in 1690 in Boston by Benjamin Harris under the title *Publick Occurrences Both Forreign and Domestick*. The paper noted that it was to be "furnished once a month (or if any Glut of Occurrences happen, oftener)."

Unfortunately it was suppressed by the government after the first number. The first continuously published American newspaper was John Campbell's Boston *News-Letter,* though it too had occasional suspensions.

From the enactment of the Stamp Act to the end of the revolution, colonial journalism became more interested in the American political scene, although news from abroad dominated most papers. Then, during the revolution itself, the politicians learned the usefulness of the press in propagandizing their particular point of view. Not a few left their journalistic stamp. The most famous Royalist editor was James Rivington, publisher of the New York *Gazeteer.* The Pennsylvania *Evening Post,* the Boston *Post-Boy,* the *Royal American Gazette* and others with names similar to the latter were all good Tory newspapers. On the other hand, Thomas Paine, the pamphleteer, writing in the *Pennsylvania Journal,* John Holt's New York *Journal,* the Boston *Spy* and the *Gazette* and many others, took the patriot's side in the North.

In the South, John Holt's *Virginia Gazette* and William Goddard's *Maryland Journal* spoke for American freedom, as did Peter Timothy's *South Carolina Gazette,* the strongest patriot crusader in the South. In some cases, as with the *Georgia Gazette,* later the *Royal Georgia Gazette,* and the *South Carolina and American General Gazette,* later the *Royal Gazette,* others remained loyal despite the reality of probable extinction. But in these early days in the nation-aborning, the divisions were not sectional. An editor and his backers were either for freedom or against it, whether they were a Jefferson or a Washington or a Randolph of Virginia, or an Adams or a Monroe, preaching what amounted to sedition in the market places and through the printing houses of the various colonies. The uncompromising divisions that rent asunder what God and the fathers of the revolution would put together were inherent in possible interpretations of the Constitution they produced, but the issue which would rend the nation was not at first apparent.

It was the very economic progress and physical growth of the United States which aggravated the tensions that led to civil war. Along the way politicians and newspaper editors as well as common citizens concerned themselves with the Missouri Compromise, what to do with the Indians, establishment of a national bank, internal improvements, the annexation of Texas and the Mexican War, the Oregon question, the Compromise of 1850, the Kansas-Nebraska Act, and a host of other political-economic issues connected with the search for fulfillment of a new country's needs. Whigs as well as Jacksonian Democrats fought over the merits of their respective parties. In the 1850s there arose, too, that motley grouping which, lumped together, was known as the Know-Nothings, whose concern had nothing to do with the fate of slavery but rather with that of another cheap form of labor, the rapidly-swelling number of immigrants, most of them impoverished Irish Roman Catholics. In these new ethnic groups the Know Nothings found a threat to the established Protestant order.

And while the editorial issues multiplied, the press was strengthened as it learned new techniques. Some newspapers did far more than creditable reporting jobs as did the New Orleans *Picayune* during the Mexican War when its George W. Kendall proved to be one of the first great war correspondents who deserves the appellation modern in a struggle which itself had its domestic origins in slavery.

Francis Lumsden, a co-founder of the *Times Picayune,* was another outstanding reporter of that war, the first ever to be covered in a comprehensive manner. Perhaps one reason for this full coverage was the intense competition among the city's eight newspapers. And from New Orleans, geographically the center for distribution of war news throughout the continent, dispatches could be sent all over the country.

The newsmen showed great imagination in getting their copy back to the home offices. Couriers, operating as the pony express did, relayed the war reports from the interior through guerrilla-infested mountains and out to the sea. From Tampico and Vera Cruz and Point Isabel, ships—sometimes specially chartered ones—would bring the news to the Crescent City. In the Civil War, the Memphis *Appeal* would set up composing rooms in box cars, but this war saw them set up in steamships that plied the waters of the Gulf of Mexico.

But the issues of slavery and states' rights were editorially paramount in the Southern press for much of the thirty years before war came. While they were not the only issues, the Southern editors, and to a greater extent the political spokesmen of states' rights, had all but prepared the region for armed civil conflict long before it came. John Brown himself was but an echo, this one from the vengeful Northern Abolitionists, of the spirit of the angry voices that would not be hushed and for whose silencing too few leaders spoke. In the South the clamor of the Rhetts and indomitable Edmund Ruffin of South Carolina, agricultural experimental genius and near-mad secessionist, and their ideological kinsmen might have been muted by stronger voices; but they were not. They remained instead the lead voices of the chorus which drowned out the spokesmen for compromise.

Then came the election of the rail-splitter from Illinois, Abraham Lincoln. Over a divided democracy and the avalanche of secession came Lincoln's call for troops and the red specter of the four horsemen against the Southern sky. The war for which some of the press of the South had so ardently spoken became a four-year holocaust and a century of paying the Northern piper in the debased coinage of the gutted South.

In the days of the Abolitionist strife that preceded actual civil war, it was some of the South's newspaper editors no less than its more fiery politicians who kept the region in ferment, a ferment in which, however, there could be no questioning of the institution of slavery as it existed within the South. Nat Turner's revolt had settled that when most of the Southern states passed their gag laws to control publication of any material which might be construed as inciting the slaves to rebellion. As for publications critical of the "peculiar institution" printed outside of the South, their circulation within the area had early been minimized. The postmasters of many Southern towns refused to deliver anti-slavery newspapers such as William Lloyd Garrison's Boston *Liberator,* the Utica *Standard* and *Democrat,* the Philadelphia (Pennsylvania) *Freeman,* the Cincinnati *Philanthropist,* and the Lexington *True American,* believing them to be "incendiary publications". Even a United States postmaster general, Amos Kendall, a former newspaperman himself, in his annual report in 1835 argued for empowering the post office to stop circulation of the "obnoxious papers" in the South. President Jackson followed up this recommendation with a similar proposal to Congress which finally resulted in a bill forbidding Abolitionist newspapers to be circulated by mail in those states which had laws against it, a measure defeated by only a narrow margin.

In the grim and hateful days before the war it was the Northern papers, published in far larger cities than any in the South and edited by far more brilliant men, who wrote and spoke against slavery until the Southern press quivered with the rawness of abraded flesh. Never before had such a galaxy shone above the Northern vineyard:

the incomparable Horace Greeley of the New York *Tri-bune,* Henry J. Raymond of the New York *Times,* James Gordon Bennett of the New York *Herald,* Samuel Bowles of the Philadelphia *Press,* Joseph Medill of the Chicago *Tribune,* William Cullen Bryant of the New York *Evening Post,* and the Abolitionist, William Lloyd Garrison.

Too many Southern editors in the pre-war and immediate post-war periods used their emotions instead of their educations. It was not an atmosphere in which detached journalism could flourish. The best that could be said for most of these editors, and it was a good best, was that they were courageous men, felt fiercely loyal to their region, and almost always were gifted with a penchant for the colorful phrase. Perhaps the principal handicaps of the Southern editor, save for a handful, were lack of capital, lack of education, and lack of communities really large enough for publication of metropolitan newspapers. This was not always true, of course. Such highly informative publications as *DeBow's Review,* published by a highly gifted man of non-sectional interests, rank with the best economic publications in the nation. So did the papers of Richmond and Louisville, the Memphis *Appeal,* and, for a while, one of the newspapers of Raleigh until their tempers got the better of the Southern editors.

Much of the defense of the South's implacable opposition was written in the blood of forgotten small-town country editors who looked upon every criticism of the South's "sacred institution" as a slur to be avenged. But the Southern duelist editors did not confine their antagonism to the Abolitionist foe. There is hardly a town of any consequence prior to, during, or after the Civil War in which some editor does not lie buried because of political conviction or political difference. But not all of the issues had to do with politics. Southern editors seemingly killed each other at times for the simple joy of it or to avenge a maligned member of the weaker sex or would shoot it out with fellow townsmen who fancied themselves libeled or whom the editors believed had slandered them. Although it will not be found in the *Guinness Book of Records,* the Vicksburg *Sentinel* set a record of sorts by having four editors killed "in personal combat" at this time. Another drowned himself, still another was imprisoned, and others were wounded.   •

Mark Twain in one part of his short story entitled "Journalism in Tennessee" recalls the newspapermen of the pre-war years and their famous imbroglios when he has the old editor, fresh from a shooting, counsel the young man who will be in charge of the office for a while:

Jones will be here at three—cowhide him. Gillespie will call earlier, perhaps—throw him out of the window. Ferguson will be along about four—kill him. That is all for today, I believe. If you have any odd time, you may write a blistering article on the police. The cowhides are under the table, weapons in the drawer, ammunition there in the corner, lint and bandages up there in the pigeonholes. In case of accident, go to Lancet, the surgeon, downstairs. He advertises; we take it out in trade.

The pre-war and war periods were violent in any case and violence was prevalent for the greater part of fifty years. The basic tragedy was that the embryonic editor needed only the proverbial shirttail of type, a composing stone or two, a desk or tables for himself and his very few assistants. Ability was secondary and even tertiary. The necessities were courage, a hot temper, regional devotion, and a loaded derringer. They had one thing in common: they were united in their hatred of Abolitionism. There were some rare exceptions, notably in east Tennessee where the Quaker Elihu Embree began the first of all American newspapers devoted entirely to the cause of Abolition, the *Emancipator.*

Some of the old-time Southern editors thought of themselves as inheritors of the mantle of Cato, who thundered *Carthago Delenda Est.* (Carthage was delenda-ested all right, but it was the Southern part of town.) Others considered themselves members of an odd sort of journalistic judiciary. Still others believed themselves humorists.

Indeed, no discussion of Southern newspapers before the war would be complete without mention of the humorous stories that their editors printed and encouraged. They were not written by professional authors, but by lawyers, doctors and others, usually cultivated men of the Southern frontier, as well as by the editors themselves. They were very realistic portrayals of the people described in contrast to the fictional literature of the period which sought to romanticize the South and its people. The men of these humorous sketches were rough-and-tumble Southerners who cursed and drank and fought and gambled fiercely. The stories portray for us today the non-political as well as political side of life in the South and, as wholly sectional humor, had great influence on later Southern writers from Mark Twain even to and beyond William Faulkner.

The first book of these sketches to be collected and published was *Georgia Scenes* by a native Georgian. Augustus Baldwin Longstreet was the author, although he published under a pseudonym as was the custom. As he was the editor of the Augusta *States Rights Sentinel,* many of the sketches had appeared in that journal first during the period 1832 to 1835, the year that the book was published.

A co-editor of Longstreet's on the *Sentinel,* William Tappan Thompson, later became editor of the *Southern Miscellany* and in that organ published a series of letters supposedly coming from Major Joseph Jones, Esq. and concerned with his courtship of his neighbor, Miss Mary

Stallins. It is not as rough as Longstreet's *Scenes* are, but
it too gives the modern reader a good idea of the life and
manners of that time, and very humorously too. These
sketches, better than any other source, give a true record
of the dialect spoken in different parts of the South at
that time. The dialect seems only vaguely related to our
modern Southern English. Take for example the description of himself by the Tennessee mountaineer, Sut Lovingood, a character created by George Washington Harris.
This description and other stories about Sut were collected in *Sut Lovingood Yarns,* an anthology which was
published in 1867 although Harris had written the individual stories for Southern newspapers, mostly prior to
the Civil War:

Every critter what hes ever seed me, ef he has sence enuff
to hide from a cummin kalamity, ur run from a muskit, jis'
knows five great facks in my case es well es they knows the
road to their moufs. *Fustly,* that I haint got nara a soul, nuf-
fin but a whisky proof gizzard, sorter like the wus half ove a
ole par ove saddil bags, *Seconly,* that I'se too durn'd a fool
to cum even onder millertary lor. *Thudly,* that I hes the
longes' par ove laigs ever hung to eny cackus, 'sceptin' only
ove a grandaddy spider, an' kin beat *him* a usen ove em jis'
es bad es a skeer'd dog kin beat a crippled mud turkil. *Foufly,*
that I kin chamber more cork-screw kill-devil whisky, an' stay
on aind, than enything 'sceptin' only a broad bottum'd chun.
Fivety, and las'ly, kin git intu more durn'd misfortnit skeery
scrapes, than enybody, an' then run outen them faster, by
golly, nor enybody.

Harris was a contemporary of Longstreet and Thomp-
son and other early Southern humorists such as Johnson
Jones Hooper, who wrote the Simon Suggs stories and T.
A. Burke who wrote *Polly Peachblossom's Wedding.* Wil-
liam T. Porter, editor of the *Spirit of the Times,* a New
York paper that reprinted many of the best Southern

sketches, published several very highly successful anthologies of these tales.

The editors stole these stories freely from other papers. One of them that made the rounds again and again was the story of Cousin Sally Dilliard, written by Hamilton C. Jones. It first appeared in the early thirties and was republished in the *Spirit of the Times* in 1844 with this preface:

We think it high time that Cousin Sally Dilliard, Captain Rice, and Mose were again brought to the memory of the public; they deserve to be brought before the public every few years. Especially will they keep our friends in good humor with themselves for at least a week after reading.

By publication of these humorous stories, so very definitely the product of their environment, the Southern editor made his newspaper that much more closely identified with the section in which he published.

So what precisely was it that the ante-bellum Southern newspapers did but fight a war before it started? Most certainly they weren't all committed to what would be considered later the cause of the South. Among those who differed were William Swain's Greensborough (North Carolina) *Patriot*. Swain eloquently defended freedom of the press, when in the early 1830s North Carolina passed laws which were designed to suppress anti-slavery newspapers. He wrote:

Before we will relinquish our right to think, speak, print, and publish our own deliberate opinions in relation to *public* men and *public* measures, we will renounce existence itself. Take away our rights as a free man and life has no charm for us! We shall deal plainly with the people, not caring who may be affected by our course. We would rather bask for one hour in the approving smiles of an intelligent and undeceived people, than to spend a whole eternity amidst the damning grins of a motley crew of office hunters, despots, demagogues, tyrants, fools, and hypocrites.

There was also Cassius Clay's *True American,* which was published in Lexington, Kentucky. He did, on occasion, print violent editorials and many that offended his neighbors. Here is an excerpt from one such editorial that Clay printed on August 12, 1845:

But, remember, you who dwell in marble palaces—that there are strong arms and fiery hearts, and iron pikes in the streets, and panes of glass only between them and the silver plate on the board and the smooth skin woman on the ottoman—when you have mocked at virtue and denied the agency of God in the affairs of men and made rapine your honied faith; tremble for the day of retribution is at hand—*and the masses will be avenged.*

Shortly thereafter, while Clay was ill his press was impounded. It was another Southern blow at freedom of the press in regard to the question of emancipation.

But there was also the Charleston *Mercury* whose objective was to "fire the Southern heart" to end its "subserviency to the North," and the Charleston *Courier* which, as the war began, summed up its editorial position:

The sword must cut asunder the last tie that bound us to a people, whom, in spite of wrongs and injustice wantonly inflicted through a long series of years, we had not yet utterly hated and despised. The last expiring spark of affection must be quenched in blood. Some of the most splendid pages in our glorious history must be blurred. A blow must be struck that would make the ears of every Republican fanatic tingle, and whose dreadful effects will be felt by generations yet to come. We must transmit a heritage of rankling and undying hate to our children.

The Pre-Civil War Southern-born editor was frequently a violent man and he was more often than not a rural untutored man. The Northern-born or Northernraised editor of a Southern newspaper was generally Unionist in his sympathies and championed democratic reforms and a free system of public education, both unusual Southern journalistic programs before the war. But probably in economic self-defense he, like the native-born editor, upheld the attitudes of community and region on the all-important issue of slavery, defending the right of men to own their fellow man no matter what the rest of the nation or world might say. One outstanding example of this dichotomy was George Prentice, the Connecticut founder of the Louisville *Journal*. Although he had two sons who were Confederate officers, and constantly criticized Lincoln, he was a strong Unionist and is credited to a great extent with keeping Kentucky from seceding. Possibly the most colorful of all the Southern editors of the pre-war (and post-war too) period was Knoxville's Parson Brownlow.

The arguments for slavery were specious. Free the slaves, screamed the penny dreadfuls and small newspapers of the South, and your daughters will be marrying Negroes. They also reminded their readers that emancipation would mean the wiping out of some four-billion dollars in property and the decline of agricultural productivity and they held up Santo Domingo as an example of that decline. Moreover, the free Negro would undoubtedly end up as a voter, which would make white home rule in the South impossible.

To the goading by orthodox newspapers—if there were then such a thing as orthodoxy on either side as far as techniques were concerned—there was that added by the church press.

The churches of the North, especially the Methodist and the Congregational, had embarked upon a vendetta of their own in the name of God. Men professing to write in the name of Jesus of Nazareth called on the Abolitionists of the debated grounds and others who were no more than banditti to kill the enemy in the spirit of Jehovah, the god of wrath. There are many examples of clerical hands more familiar with type and a derringer than with a Holy Bible. Their words were daubed with the blood of fellow Christians whose sin it was to believe that a man was not doomed to hell-fire because he spoke out for states' rights and defended slavery. It was a short step from having God on your side to using God in the editorial columns to vindicate murder.

In 1860, after a mob seized and hanged the Northern Abolitionist churchman, Anthony Bewley, a Texas journal of Southern Methodism, the *Christian Advocate,* commented: "He was . . . warned by a large committee of Southern men that the anti-slavery missionary operations among us would certainly result in bloodshed and that if he persisted he would be regarded as an aggressor and treated accordingly."

And the same year, the New Orleans *Christian Advocate* roared that "Abolition doctrine has been the direct cause of both the John Brown and the Texas conspiracies, together with all similar disturbances . . . [in Texas]. The men, the old women, and the children were all to be killed, and the young women to be devoted to a far more horrible fate."

The so-called religious press became an evil travesty upon the Christian religion and the man who preached forgiveness and tolerance and understanding in Galilee.

The religious press shocked the handful who could read it with detachment. But the fulminations of the secular press were as dreadful, lacking only the hypocritical taint of pseudo-Christianity to make them as shameful as their spiritually animated counterparts published by men of the cloth, a cloth whose devout blackness bore the dull rusty red of blood. And so the rumblings of the skies grew louder and louder as the intersectional barrage of words mounted.

The editor of the Boston *Times* chose the population of New Orleans as his target. They were "an audience of slave traders with a mint julep in one hand and a Bowie knife in the other dealing in young mulattresses for the seraglios." The New Orleans *Daily Picayune* labelled it a "scurrilous attack" and called Abolition "a stain upon the nineteenth century". Behind the pages of the newspapers their readers all but foamed at the mouth.

Then a Creole general from New Orleans, a dapper West Pointer named Beauregard, gave the order from Charleston. Cannon spoke and a war began. It was a war that would not end until over three-quarters of a million Americans lay in their graves.

What then, in illogical order, was the impact of the Southern press upon the imminent reality of war? Certainly paramount was the role of some of the Southern journals as irreconcilable spokesmen of hate and suspicion and defiance of the rest of the nation. Next must be listed the defensive identification with the prevailing Southern desire to bring matters to a head, even if it took a war to make the point. The third was a spirit of braggadocio which characterized the frontier South as it does any frontier, and which impelled the Southern journalist to write, believing that what he was writing was gospel, that "One Southerner could whip ten Yankees."

Perhaps apocryphal but illustrative of this spirit was the dialogue between a somewhat chastened fire-eater and the reader-warrior who took his editor seriously, too seriously. They met soon after Appomattox, the veteran saying to the editor, "Wasn't it you who told us back in '61 that we could whip the Yankees with a bundle of crab-

apple switches?" "Maybe I did," answered the editorialist,
"Yep, I reckon I did . . . and what happened? Those
yellow cowards wouldn't fight us that way!"

It is probably unfair to describe the Southern newspapers as being principally responsible because of their
vituperation and their talent for arousing Southern tempers and Southern fears. But it is undoubtedly true that
the most notable and tragic contribution of the Southern
newspapers to the direction that the South took in the
pre-war generation was their grim talent for leading the
white South to the Armageddon that was spelled Appomattox and which left the South economically and politically and emotionally crippled. It was not a happy contribution.

TWO

The Fighting Cocks

EVEN HAD THERE BEEN NO NEWSPAPERS IN THE SOUTH OR
North to rouse their readers to frenzy the Civil War
would have been fought just the same. The adversaries
had gone too far—partly through pride, partly through
anger, partly through fear—to turn back. They looked
with outrage across the Potomac, swearing from the one
side that the Yankees of the North and from the other that
the slavocracy of the South would never be able to accommodate to each other's points of view. They never found
out whether they could or not for the hounds of war were
baying too close at one another's heels in 1860 to make
possible any successful search for peaceful compromise.
Both sides were spurred by the ghosts of John Brown's
men and the stench of blood in murderous Kansas, the
caning in Congress of Charles Sumner by Preston Brooks
of South Carolina who thus sought to avenge a slur on a
kinsman, the kidnappings, the murders, the bushwhack-
ing, and the underground railroad. The United States by
1860 was already at war with itself without knowing it.
And neither the Southern press nor the newspapers of
the North helped matters.

The schism between North and South—and between
secessionist and pro-slavery newspapers and loyalists—

19

broke into the open with the Compromise of 1850, which was endorsed by most Whig journals and repudiated by most Democratic journals. In Georgia the *Southern Banner* and the *Cassville Standard* were the only two Democratic newspapers to endorse the Compromise. The *Banner's* Hopkins Holsey, probably the most courageous Unionist editor in Georgia, and one of the most courageous in the South, withstood enemy efforts at intimidation. So also did Dr. L. F. W. Andrews, editor of the *Macon Citizen* who carried on an unending battle for freedom of the press. At the other extreme was the *Federal Union* which demanded that all reporters from outside the state be barred from writing in Georgia newspapers.

Especially violent and dangerous to continuance of the Union were such of the Southern papers that early took the adamant position that secession was the only solution. Such a one—and the most virulent—was Robert Barnwell Rhett's Charleston *Mercury* which had advocated nullification as early as 1832 and progressed rapidly to saying that the Union must go. In 1860 Rhett wrote, "For the last ten years the people of South Carolina have thought the dissolution of the Union afforded the only adequate remedy to check Northern aggression upon the South, and to secure Southern institutions and civilization from the fierce and increasing assaults of that inimical section."

Rhett, a South Carolina statesman, finding himself rebuked in the early fifties, relaxed his efforts for a while until he became alarmed about the rising power of the National Democrats in South Carolina. He, William L. Yancey, and other fire-eaters met in Montgomery to map plans for a secessionist victory which they believed must come soon or never. Paradoxically they believed that only a Republican victory in 1860 could achieve their goal. Such a victory they hoped would arouse and demoralize the South to such an extent that in its immediate wake they could call for secession before the South had become balanced again.

The *Mercury* deviously supported the Democratic party formally while fulminating against its leaders and actions in such a way as to destroy its solidarity. This was, of course, finally achieved with the split at the Charleston convention.

Not satisfied that the nation was permanently divided even after South Carolina's secession and that of the other states making up the Confederate convention, the *Mercury* called urgently for strengthening of the Confederacy in the fear that a reconstruction of the nation might be achieved if the North made concessions. Rhett urged as another block to reunion a prompt Confederate offensive. When this was delayed, the *Mercury* charged that Jefferson Davis, the president of the new Southern Confederacy, had ordered the postponement in the hope that reconciliation might be effected.

Other Southern papers supporting secession early were the Savannah *Republican* and the Natchez *Free Trader* which thought secession the method prescribed by the Constitution to remedy such wrongs as those suffered by the South.

But the majority of the Southern press had not contemplated disunion with equanimity. The Whig papers of the forties and fifties, such as the Richmond *Whig,* had decried such a solution, and the Memphis *Inquirer* advised each of its readers "to put his foot on disunion." Clearsightedly realistic, the Mobile *Advertiser,* the New Orleans *Bulletin,* the Nashville *Banner,* and the Natchez *Courier* warned of the South's dependence on the industrial North for many of its supplies, a dependence which these papers realized made resistance futile.

Some fought secession to the very end. The North Carolina *Standard* for instance condemned the firing on Fort

Sumter and reluctantly consented to war only "if it be forced upon the South." The New Orleans *Bee* went even further in support of peace and after Lincoln's election still called for the South's "unconditional submission" to the Union.

The coming of the war posed physical problems for the editors and their papers. The Southern press had its own heroic fighters, its own proud moments and days and even months. Consider the undaunted hegira of the Memphis *Appeal* which quit that city just before its fall and for more than three years was to live on the run—its safest stop, as it turned out, at Macon. With battle raging on the Mississippi river at Memphis, the editor loaded his press and type into a box car and published for a few months at Grenada, from which the *Appeal* fled to Jackson, Mississippi, until it was shelled out of that city. It then moved by rail to Atlanta, then to Montgomery, then to Columbia, where the proof-press and some of the type which were left were destroyed by Union forces. The press itself and the rest of the cases of type were spirited into a safe hideaway at Macon from which they did not emerge until after General Sherman had ordered that destruction of public property should cease. With Appomattox the paper promptly returned to Memphis and valiantly began publication again in November.

Those editors who were able to continue publication without moving had to contend with the shortage of newsprint. The classic substitute was wallpaper and today authentic copies of the Vicksburg *Daily Citizen* printed on wallpaper in the last days of the siege are collectors' items. Imitations of this ingenious means of publication are sold widely, but the authentic editions are rare indeed.

Many other Southern newspapers were forced to print wallpaper editions. Among these were the *Pictorial Democrat* and the *Southern Sentinel* of Alexandria, Louisiana, the *Courier* of St. Martinville and the *Stars and Stripes* of Thibodeaux. Other journals were just as short of supplies and had to publish on paper bags, stationery, and even everyday wrapping paper or not print at all. The warning of the New Orleans *Bulletin,* which had suggested that the Southern newspapers shouldn't talk too much about secession when they still used Northern type and presses and ink and of course paper, proved to be true. Some of the few paper mills which had been set up in the South and which produced a low grade of newsprint were accidentally or purposefully destroyed by the enemy.

Even before the newspapers resorted to wallpaper and wrapping paper, they were almost all forced to make their editions smaller. The Charleston *Courier's* course was typical. On September 1, 1861, it reduced the size of its pages to 18 inches by 26 inches. Four months later, it reduced them to 15x24 and three months later it further reduced them to 13x20. It finally ended up as a single sheet only 10 inches by 15 inches with only four columns to a page. Because they took up too much valuable space, headlines had been scrapped along with regular-sized type.

Even though editions were often limited to one small page, high rates had to be charged. The Macon *Daily Telegraph,* which by 1864 had a subscription price of $48 a year, was asking $120 a year at the end of the war while the *Georgia Journal and Messenger,* also published at Macon, charged $72 a year from the beginning of the war and more later.

On top of the high subscription and single-copy charge there was, as always in times of shortage, extortionate profiteering. In the case of newspapers it was by the street sellers. The *Citizen* at Vicksburg felt obliged to explain, printing the following notice:

"The price of our paper at the office is twenty-five cents.

Newsboys who charge fifty cents on the streets are not authorized by us to sell at that price; and those who object to the extortion should call at the office and get their papers at first cost. We cannot control the trade nor the prices of newsboys and can only sell our papers to them at the same prices that we get from those who call at the office."

While some of the papers, especially those closest to the front lines, required payment in coin—not even in Confederate paper—the Athens (Georgia) *Southern Watchman* in an issue of May, 1865, noted that its subscription rate could be paid with "any kind of produce—corn, wheat, flour, oats, rye, butter, hay, shucks, fodder, chickens, eggs —anything that can be eaten or worn, or that will answer for fuel." Other newspapers to resort to this were the Macon *Daily Telegraph*, the Paulding (Mississippi) *Eastern Clarion*, and the Richmond *Daily Sentinel*.

For those papers falling behind enemy lines, shortages were the least of their problems.

The clandestine newspapers of the Confederacy, most of them published behind enemy lines or within them after Union Troops overran and occupied much of the Southern territory, afford proud proof of the unconquerable spirit of man. In suburban Richmond, near surrounded Nashville and Atlanta, and in New Orleans, the printing presses of the South carried on the battle and they pulled no punches. *Le Carillon,* one of the French newspapers of New Orleans wrote of General Butler, "What belly has vomited you forth, in what den were you conceived, how could so scaly a reptile not rend your mother's entrails when you were born?" Friends who wished to save the Creole editor shortly whisked him away to safety in France.

If the newspapers of the South's occupied cities published anything that the general in charge thought was treasonous, the paper would be suspended or the writer of the editorial or news report would be forced to resign from the paper, or the newspaper itself, in some cases, would be turned over to Northern newspapermen to edit. An example of the latter was the *Daily Argus* of Memphis, which offended General Wallace by publishing a report which was false and which he labeled false—the capture of Cincinnati by Confederate troops. The general appointed A. G. Richardson, a correspondent of the New York *Tribune,* and Thomas W. Knox of the New York *Herald* to take over publication of the paper. In another incident involving a Memphis newspaper, the *Avalanche* was ordered by General Grant to either suspend publication or to fire Jeptha Folkes, the author of an editorial entitled "Mischief-Makers" which appeared in the paper and which the general considered treasonable. In New Orleans several newspapers including the *Bee,* the *Delta* and the *Crescent* were thought guilty of treason and were suspended at various times. On the other hand, when federal troops occupied Knoxville, Parson Brownlow, a Union sympathizer who had published there prior to Confederate occupation of the city, was able to renew operation of his newspaper again, this time under the title of *Whig and Rebel Ventilator.*

Today a Communist enemy would line captured editors up before firing squads. The Germans and the Russians of World War II did not hesitate to murder such journalists as those of the clandestine press. They were the enemy and the enemy must be destroyed. But this was a different kind of war, perhaps the last in which certain rules of military conduct or fair play were observed more often than not. In this vanishing orthodoxy Southern editors in conquered territory were fortunate. Their property would be confiscated, of course. They would be hailed before military courts for drumhead court martials. They

would be sentenced to military prisons, though not for
long; and very few Southern editors remained in prison
after Appomattox. But with some glaring and bloody
exceptions, the men who fought the American Civil War
demonstrated a decency of conduct, a treatment of foemen on the battlefield and in the printing shop that the
world was not to see again.

The Northern army frequently used equipment taken
from printing plants in the Confederate towns that they
captured to print newspapers for the soldiers. When the
Third Iowa Regiment entered the town of Macon, Missouri, it used the type and presses of that town's *Register*
to print its own organ, the *Union,* and Wilson's troops
did the same in Macon, Georgia. Other Northern army
papers published for various periods of time on presses
earlier devoted to the Southern cause were the Port Hud-
son *Freeman,* the *Kettle-Drum,* and one of the best, the
Weekly Junior Register, which General Banks issued after
the capture of Franklin, Louisiana.

The Confederacy also published papers for its troops.
Joseph W. Tucker, a Methodist preacher and a former
editor of the St. Louis *Missouri State Journal,* edited
the *Missouri Army Organ* for the army of the state. It was
first published at Neosho on October 28, 1861, and was
paid for by the state. Camp Churchill Clark near Corinty,
Arkansas, saw the last issue of the little paper. The *Rebel
and Copperhead Ventilator,* in some aspects an army
paper, was also published in Missouri at Edina. The most
famous of the Confederate army organs was the *Vidette,*
which was published by General Morgan's men. Others
were the *Free Speech Advocate,* the *Daily Rebel Banner*
and the *Missouri Army Argus.* The *Army Argus and
Critic,* which was published in Mobile, was primarily for
the military. It carried news of the war along with cas-
ualty lists.

If no printing presses were available, the soldiers' thirst for news was quenched by newspapers issued in manuscript, with such names as "The Rapid Ann," "The Mule," and "The Woodchuck."

If the Southern press was emotional before the war, it cloyed the senses beyond any justification during the conflict. It is axiomatic that the soldier who fights on his own soil, the householder who looks upon the ashes of his home, the journalist who rarely has any true victory about which to brag will be more venomous and uncompromising and furious in his wrath than one who possesses the field of battle and burned the houses and destroyed the newspaper's type. It is understandable too that the editor will blame a retreating friend more than the successful enemy. He expects in the ally an invincibility that no one can really possess, and he does not willingly attribute the success of the enemy to numbers and supplies. Thus almost no Southern general escaped the wrath of the South's beleaguered journals; certainly no politicians did, nor did many of them deserve to go unscathed.

It is a strange contradiction that the Southern newspapers which by their virulent and frequently unjustified condemnation of the South's political and military leaders contributed to the defeat of the Confederacy itself, strengthened the American concept of freedom of the press by these criticisms and by demanding the right to criticize. In the long run this meant more to the cause of freedom of expression and therefore to the cause of the bill of rights than did anything to come out of the conflict.

In the North Lincoln's administration curtailed the journalistic freedom of at least two-dozen newspapers because they exercised what they thought to be their inalienable right, even in time of strife: that of criticism of the conduct of the war and individual war leaders. Although it is true that in 1864 Jefferson Davis sought an act giving

three-year control of the press and that two years earlier
the Confederate States' House Military Committee wanted
penalties imposed for the leaking of information about
the army's operations, the Southern press remained rela-
tively, even absolutely, free. Some restrictions were imposed on field correspondents and a few newspapers were
occasionally suppressed for rallying the planters to anti-
government causes, but there was no comparison between
the extent of Southern and Union control of the press.

From the beginning the Northern generals were not at
all pleased with the Northern newspaper correspondents'
handling of war news. Early in the war, in August 1861,
General McClellan held a conference with newsmen advising them about the difficulties implicit in covering the
war. A resolution was passed at the meeting requesting
the government to set up facilities for giving out information about war activities. But the newsmen were too eager
to wait for official information. So anxious were they to
scoop one another's papers that the generals soon placed
restrictions on the areas in which the correspondents could
operate and tried to hold the editors responsible for what
their newsmen reported. The Northern generals wanted
published only news of what had already taken place, not
information on maneuvers in progress, fearing that ad-
vantages of secrecy and concentration would be negated.
Complaints by generals were widespread.

In 1862 Confederate Secretary of War Randolph said
that he hoped "this revolution may be successfully closed
without suppression of one single newspaper in the Confederate States, and that our experience may be able to
challenge comparison with our enemy." He had the satisfaction of knowing that not one newspaper in the South
was ever suppressed, even for short periods, by either the
state or Confederate governments. And Davis himself,
though the target of many vitriolic attacks, ardently de-

fended the right of the press to attack even him. For more
would be lost than gained, he felt, in suppressing the
newspapers. In the beginning it was left to the reporter's
own discretion and honor not to publish information that
might give aid and comfort to the Northern enemy.
Improper information was not to be allowed to pass
through the telegraph wires, but even this mild form of
censorship was almost nonexistent.

Complaints about the press by generals were not limited
to those by Northern officers, however. Eventually such
Confederate military leaders as Joseph E. Johnston, Bragg,
Beauregard, and Jackson made their own encampments off
limits to Southern reporters. They too claimed that the
enemy knew of their plans because of the press. Indeed,
they were probably right, for it was not uncommon for
the newspapers to publish Confederate plans of attack.
The editors felt they had the right to publish anything
that they chose. As the Charleston *Courier* noted, freedom
of the press was "really threatened more by the reckless
abuse and excessive license practiced by some of its advo-
cates and expounders" than by any form of government
suppression.

Principal target of the Southern editors was the president of the Confederacy, who was repeatedly identified as
that "vast complication of incompetence and folly" by the
Charleston *Mercury,* which also excoriated the Confederate generals. The Richmond *Examiner* was the Virginia
paper making the most malicious attacks upon Davis and
his administration. Other papers which followed suit
were the *Whig* and the *Enquirer,* the *Dispatch* and the
Sentinel, all of Richmond, though the latter two were not
as savage. Off and on, with changing issues, the Lynchburg
Virginian, the Memphis *Appeal,* the Atlanta *Southern
Confederacy,* the Macon *Intelligencer,* the Macon *Telegraph,* the Columbus *Sun,* the Augusta *Chronicle and Sen-*

tinel, the Savannah *Republican* castigated the Confederate government. Rhett's *Mercury* needed no special issue but continuously lambasted the administration.

William W. Holden's Raleigh *Standard* went so far as to be considered treasonable in its attacks. It was held in such low regard that its offices were sacked by the Georgia Brigade when that military unit passed through town. Not to be outdone, supporters of the *Standard* did the same to the Raleigh *State Journal,* whose editorial policies were in contrast to those of the *Standard.*

At the same time that the Southern press was condemning the South's leaders, her newspapers were building up her victories out of all proportion to reality. This wishful thinking had some curious results, such as the annihilation of Grant's troops at Vicksburg by a Jackson news correspondent. Some insignificant skirmishes were played up as "glorious news" or "brilliant victories."

I remember the allied propagandists of World War I who shocked and probably titillated their readers with their accounts of the old Hun custom of slicing off the bosoms of beautiful Belgian women. They had their counterparts in Southern editors propagandizing for the South. The Richmond *Examiner* wrote of Union men: "Brutal soldiery, drunken with wine, blood and fury . . . [who enter] every dwelling at their pleasure, plunder the property, ravish the women, burn the house, and proceed to the next." The Augusta *Register* reported that those "incarnate devils," Sherman's troops, "ravished some of the nicest ladies of the town" in Milledgeville, Georgia.

According to the Southern press the Southern prisoners of war were treated as badly. Clement Eaton has pointed out that "In general, the degree of atrocity seemed to vary in inverse ratio with the fortunes of the Confederacy."

Sometimes exaggerated or totally false reporting was deliberate. The most notable such case was the brain-

child of Robert E. Lee himself who used the Richmond
papers to deceive the North's general, George B. McClellan, his principal adversary in the field. McClellan accepted as military gospel false reports which Lee had
requested the *Whig* and *Enquirer* to publish, all to the
Confederacy's advantage.

Southern readers hardly knew when to believe their
newspapers, and newspaper editors their correspondents.
Almost all newspaper subscribers were familiar with the
headlines "Important—If True." The Baltimore *Sun* took
note of the "credibility gap" in its issue of May 27, 1861,
when it front-paged an article entitled "Rumors and
Speculations": "Rumors of every kind multiply. Every
hour gives rise to the most extravagant reports. The
press, North and South, seems to have entered upon a war
of crimination and recrimination, and instead of calming
the excitement and allaying unfounded prejudice, to rejoice in adding to the excitement of the moment." But
few were such rational thinkers.

We tend to overlook the good reporting that came out
of the Civil War, and there was some very good reporting indeed, although more of it was for the Northern papers. Probably the Civil War allowed more first-hand,
close-to-the-battle reporting than has been possible in any
later war, although much of the copy was late—three or
four days at the least, several weeks at the most—and it
was very hard come by. Unlike contemporary wars, the
Civil War did not recognize correspondents or "specials"
as they were called, as noncombatants, so they were more
subject to the realities of death on the battlefield than
those who would report later wars.

There were countless stories of courageous "specials"
who weathered battles, military prisons, and the embattled telegraph lines to get their copy in. Northern correspondents frequently had to bring their copy personally

by train to their home offices because the lines would be closed to them, a form of censorship by the military. Whitelaw Reid's reporting of the Battle of Bull Run is considered among the classics of war reporting. Murat Halstead, John Russell Young, and Henry Villard were all good reporters during war time.

The Southern papers relied principally on officers and even some privates to supply them with old but usually lively copy of the war. One amateur on-the-scene reporter was John Esten Cooke, later a Southern novelist, who was attached to the Army of Northern Virginia and who chronicled it, if unobjectively, nevertheless with unsurpassed insight, for the Richmond *Southern Illustrated News*.

How to assemble news of the cities and towns of the Confederacy, in addition to battlefield coverage, called for some form of joint undertaking.

At the beginning of the war, in the fall of 1862, four of the Richmond papers formed the Mutual Benefit Press Association, with J. W. Lewellen as president. In return for all the latest news from the capital, members were expected to pay $5 a month and contribute important news from their own localities. It was not a serious rival of the Confederate Press Association which was founded a few months later.

Another local group was the Weekly Press Association of Georgia founded in April 1863. Its main purpose was to set uniform prices for subscriptions, advertisements, and the like. Weekly papers had unusual difficulty in collecting news since the Confederate Press Association did not serve them. Besides many newspapers did not have telegraphic connections (none of the Texas newspapers did). They copied much of the war news from the association papers despite the copyright in some instances.

The Press Association of the Confederate States was organized in February 1863 in Augusta, Georgia, after two

previous attempts at organization had failed. It was formed
in part as a protest against the news agency that operated
out of Richmond which was controlled by William H.
Pritchard, who had represented the New York Associated
Press before the Civil War. It was felt that the arrange-
ment aided Pritchard too much instead of being mutually
beneficial.

The new mutual press association immediately came to
be the primary one, with Dr. R. W. Gibbs as president
and J. S. Thrasher as general manager. Its correspondents
covered every place of importance in the Confederacy, and
local papers sent in news of those places that were not
covered. Members were assured of exclusive news stories
because the material was copyrighted. They were also assured of fresh news stories, and many newspapermen mar-
velled at the speed with which information was received.
The association had worked out an agreement with the
telegraph company that allowed its material to travel at
half the rate charged private individuals. But only the
most important words were transmitted in copy, so that
many editors complained that the association's releases
were gibberish.   (Other newspapers complained that too
many trivial incidents were included in the dispatches.)
The association also published a monthly pamphlet of
current news.

There were fewer specials for the Southern papers simply because there were fewer papers, and they could ill
afford financially to keep correspondents in the field.
Then, as more and more territory fell to the North, the
North suppressed the Southern newspapers remaining in
that territory. The Union also gained control of more
telegraph lines and railways, making it very difficult to
get fresh copy to the home office. Qualified personnel
available for newspaper work lessened in the South as the
war stretched out. Southern paper mills could not meet

Southern demands for paper even during peacetime, much less during war, and the blockades kept foreign sources from supplying the region. A quotation from the Hamilton *Court-House Gazette,* in its suspension edition of June 1, 1862, sums up the difficulties encountered by the Southern newspaper: "The proprietor has been reluctantly compelled to come to this decision in consequence of the editor, the compositors and the printers have gone off to war, the devil only is left in the office."

As the war went on with a predictably hopeless outcome for the South and because of the ever more ruinous hardships of the poor Southern white, many of whom in time marked the conflict between the states as "a rich man's war and a poor man's fight," the Southern soldiers set a record for military desertion second only to that of the Northern mercenary immigrants from Germany and Ireland who took the Yankee dollar over and over again. What made the desertion more reprehensible in the South was that the Confederate soldiers were fighting in their homeland. Nothing the Southern newspapers could do by appealing to Southern patriotism could slow down this rate of desertion which was so high that even General Lee himself commented despairingly upon the disappearance of thousands of veterans from the ranks each year, especially after Gettysburg.

The South did develop a nucleus of what can only be described as magnificent fighting men who wouldn't quit. But little that the newspapers themselv greatly to the nucleus after the great defe the outnumbered and outsupplied Souther

Whatever its shortcomings the Southern mirable contributions to the theory and pr nalistic freedom. The rank and file Southe duced a largely honorable and courageous e of journalists who were more concerned w dom and its expression in time of peril than in individual or professional safety. And, whatever other criticism can be leveled, cowardice was not one of them. During the war and its aftermath of reconstruction the Southern editor behaved almost invariably with courage and usually with dignity. This was a tradition based upon the principle of personal honor which outlasted the war and which gave a dangerously heady flavor to Southern journalism. It has persisted, though with far less prevalence, to this day.

To understand the Southern press and its impact, it is necessary that we comprehend something about the Southern nation which the press helped create and which survived nationhood itself. The sentimentalist is inclined to forget the tragedy of that nation and the suffering of the men who defended it. It is easier to say simply that in the United States from 1861-1865 was fought the last of the sentimental wars by men who, believing in themselves and loving what they fought for, were the spokesmen of the American Armageddon. A man could fall down with the blood from a musket ball wound gurgling in a torn throat and in that way die happy. From the lips of the dying came the whispering of wasted courage. "Lorena" they sang, the young and the brave and the dying, and "The Yellow Rose of Texas," a popular song, from a black-face minstrel show, whose lyrics extolled the charms of a light-skinned Negro girl. The ragged columns swung down through the dusty valleys and across the mountains chanting the words of another minstrel song that would live as long as any that were sung during that war. "Dixie" its name was. (Today, 100 years after Lee's surrender, there is an almost-incendiary quality to the refrain about the mystical, mythical land of cotton whose music would outlast fact.) And around the campfires and in the sweaty wards of the charnel houses that passed for hospitals, a man who that day had cut a fellow human being's throat

from ear to ear wept over the poem about "Little Giffen"
of Tennessee.

Yes, it was a sentimental war, even a chivalric one,
where enemies could be briefly friends by night and men
fought by certain rules of the game.

But there was more to it, unhappily more, than senti-
ment and chivalry. And the South in its newspapers knew
it even better than its enemies. For what is often over-
looked is that in the South two wars were fought—one by
the organized soldiery of each side, the other by guerrillas
operating behind the lines of the orthodox enemy. This
was the war in Kentucky which produced its full quota of
rebels, in Missouri whose bushwhackers wrote probably
the cruelest chapters of the war, and in eastern Tennessee
and of that part of Virginia which by reason of its loyal
tendencies would emerge as West Virginia. It was the war
in the Appalachian mountain men who cared little or
nothing for the slave owner or secessionist but who pinned
their loyalties to John Calhoun's principle of states' rights.
This was truly the war of the brothers which is the blood-
iest of all. And in its wake, hate festered and men sought
to find something in the ashes. So this was the second war
in the Civil War itself and a case might be made for its
nature, which was more venomous and left a deeper dis-
charge of poison than ever did the larger battles.

The press of the South had to fight both wars; it was its
duty to find consolation for the troubled, fearful heart, to
assuage heartbreak and the hidden awareness of the all
but inevitable defeat. It was the white Southern press
which could rejoice too confidently in that first battle
fought in the area of a Virginia creek that the South
would remember pridefully as the Battle of Manassas. It
created the pride that the bloody standoff at Shiloh would
give to a South already beginning to realize that the nation within a nation was up against economic and man-

power odds which might be insurmountable. This Southern press tried to provide the excuses for the battles of
Gettysburg, Chattanooga, and the Wilderness; and it had
to persuade ever more disconsolate, hungry, and exhaust-
ed soldiers and civilians that they could fight another
time and win.

And when the end of the war had given the lie to the
futile hope, the Southern press, which had at first accepted the result, found it could not stomach the realities
of a Reconstruction it had not envisioned.

None of us in the United States today, save for a handful of immigrants who have come to the United States as
a beaten people, know what it is to be defeated. Some of
these political refugees have undertaken to be spokesmen
for their vanquished countries and will not accept defeat
as vindication of the victory of the triumphant foemen.
During the years of Radical Reconstruction of the South
the Southern press would for the most part take on that
same role, and the courage which had been tested in the
war years would know even greater challenge.

THREE

The Printed Word in War and Defeat

IF THE WAR BETWEEN THE STATES WAS A GRIMLY SENTI-
mental holocaust, it was also the last major conflict to be
fought with overtones of chivalry and by certain rules,
even though these were more honored in the breach than
in the observance. Prisoners did keep their paroles. What
care was available was afforded the wounded prisoners,
Camp Douglas in Chicago where some 7,000 Southern in-
mates died, and Andersonville, the most notorious camp
in the South, notwithstanding. Efforts to the limits of the
resources available were made by both sides to keep a
captive's body and soul together. But the Southern prisoners suffered intolerably, incurring many casualties because of the rigors of the unfamiliar winter. The Northern prisoners had no quarrel with the weather, but they
paid dearly for the South's lack of medicine. On both sides
of the line the presses fulminated with passion against the
shortages and shortcomings which made the prison camps
hell on earth, although their outrage did almost nothing
to aid the abused prisoners of war on either side. Some
Yankee and Rebel troops did fraternize between the lines

during a night's vigil, swapping tobacco for small luxuries and medicines. And an officer's word to his captors was his bond. No evidence exists of more than isolated incidents of rape. If great homes and small cabins alike were destroyed by Sherman's bummers, this resulted from the dictates of war and was certainly no worse or widespread than devastation in France and Germany and Russia and Coventry and the Japan of Nagasaki and Hiroshima in World Wars I and II.

Yes, as wars go, it was a decent war, the principal trouble with it being that the South lost, and in the losing a hornet's nest was stirred with such angry vigor that the vengeful buzzing would last for a hundred years, even to our own time and beyond.

It could have been different. A living Lincoln could have made Reconstruction so. Andrew Johnson could have too, had the implacable foes of a crushed South given him the opportunities. For Andrew Johnson, hard man of the people, the Unionist and commoner, foe of Southern aristocracy, loved the South of his nativity. He did what he could, but the Sumners, Stantons, and Stevenses gave him no more of a chance living than an assassin's bullet gave Abe Lincoln dead.

And so, after the first shock and the first feeble efforts toward recovery, the newspapers of the South forgot that they were, in effect, the prisoners not only of military conquerers but of new ideas and sought to raise their heads above the hills of a Rome which would never be the same.

The politicians took to the hustings. A few, like General Longstreet of Louisiana and Governors Brown of Georgia and Orr of South Carolina, changed their political allegiances to join up with the opposition for reasons that may have seemed honorable and valid to them, but which more often than not were not taken that way. Such men knew a special Gethsemane of their own and were forced to wear unfairly the Judas label and the badge of Cain.

Criticism of the military occupation and occupiers brought military action against editors who went beyond the very narrow limits permitted. One highly-controversial case was that of Colonel W. H. McCardle, the editor of the Vicksburg *Times,* who made no bones about his detestation of General Ord, the military commander of the Fourth District, and of the Republicans in Congress. In November 1867 a lieutenant led a squad of soldiers into the *Times* office, arrested the editor, and lodged him in a military prison in Jackson. Soon thereafter Colonel McCardle was tried before a military commission on charges of denouncing General Ord as a usurper and a despot, with defaming the character of an agent of the Freedmen's Bureau, and with advising voters to remain away from the polls at the time of the election at which it was to be ascertained whether a majority of Mississippians desired a convention to gain readmission as a state, all contributing to a general charge of impeding the execution of the Reconstruction laws.

Colonel McCardle applied to the United States Circuit Court for a writ of habeas corpus. At the hearing Judge Robert A. Hill held that the question involved the constitutionality of the Reconstruction Acts, decided that those acts were constitutional, that the powers vested in the commanding general had not been transcended by him, and that Colonel McCardle was subject to arrest and trial before a military commission without being indicted. Accordingly the editor was returned to the custody of the military authorities. He then appealed to the Supreme Court of the United States under a congressional act which authorized appeals in such cases; but before the Supreme Court could reach a decision Congress passed another act which deprived the court of jurisdiction.

Frequently, however, the newspaper plant of the former Confederate supporter was simply taken over by a Union sympathizer or operated as a Republican journal by the former owner. In Richmond, after the evacuation of the capital by the Confederacy, the owner who remained without editor or staff—they having departed with the Southern troops—announced that henceforward his paper would express only Union sympathies. The financial rewards of editorial support by the carpetbag-scalawag press could be great and were enhanced by the close ties between such newspapers and the Republican-dominated legislatures. Here the corruption of the press rotted the moral fiber of this brand of Southern journalism more than did any other kind of relationship. The post-war Constitutional Convention in Mississippi, which cost a quarter of a million dollars, allotted $28,518.75 to four obscure Republican papers for publishing the official proceedings. In Arkansas, where each member of the legislature was voted ten free newspaper subscriptions, the printing was let to a politician, without competition, at an astounding rate. To advertise his proclamations (as required by law) the Carpetbag governor of Georgia, Rufus B. Bullock, spent $98,000 of the state's money in just three years. From 1855 to 1860, $5,000 had been Georgia's entire expenditures for the same purpose. The opportunities presented by the printing of official proceedings were not to be matched for sixty years, when Huey Long's Louisiana machine would demonstrate that in this field it could teach the Carpetbaggers a thing or two. Obviously there was nothing new in the subterfuge and general double-dealing which transferred thousands of dollars from the public till into the journalistic coffers, but never before Reconstruction had dishonesty been made so easy. It was as if the hands of the Southern taxpayer and the members of the political minorities had been tied behind their backs while assailants engaged in free and fancy looting to their heart's content.

In Charleston such conditions made the other Charleston journals convert the motto of the carpetbag newspaper, the *South Carolina Ledger,* "Free Labor and General Reforms," to "Free Lunch and General Graft."

In 1867 the Charleston *Mercury* which had resumed publication under the leadership of its pre-war fire-eating editor, Robert Barnwell Rhett, Jr., printed sketches of the careers of the delegates to the South Carolina Reconstruction Convention, savagely caricaturing the carpetbag and Negro members. Shortly he announced that a "mongrel" government was too much for him to bear, and even though in August of 1868 his newspaper was the largest in the state in circulation, he suspended publication three months later. His reason, he wrote, was to "take his place among the ruined children of the South—better so than to be the proudest and most honored of her successful enemies—and to wait, hoping, praying, expecting the bright coming of a final deliverance, the independence and prosperity of the South."

But if the carpetbag editors rejoiced in a heyday of skulduggery, their white Democratic opponents took a revenge of sorts. They could fight only with words, but those words seared the consciences, if any there were, of their adversaries and held them up to scornful attack such as few editors would tolerate even today.

The *Mercury* of Meridian, Mississippi, stated its policy in no uncertain terms, terms which were pretty generally accepted as reflecting the attitude of most of the Southern weeklies. Newspapers, it said, "should be the masters, not the bootlicks of politicians. Let newspapers boldly cry aloud and spare not, and turn the whore of Expediency out of doors. Let us have no fornicating with the Radical

Party, under the idea of begetting a 'new South', but let us nail our colors to the mast, and stand by them like men. Nothing else will save us."

While this statement came fairly late in the Reconstruction period, the colorful rodomontade was characteristic of the more expressive weekly editors.

The weekly press, because it didn't have the news services available to the dailies, depended on its exchanges for national and international news on which to comment, and by so doing kept its readers fairly well informed of current events outside the immediate area. In addition the use of boiler plate—features cast into type by a syndicate and sold, with its advertising, to the weeklies—and of ready-print paper, one side of which came printed with similar general features, helped to round out the reading material the weeklies could offer. But the most important function of the rural press was to keep the readers in their own trade territory informed of local developments. And this they did with courage and with a high degree of integrity, that was sometimes perfervid in its expression.

And there were clandestine publications of the Ku Klux Klan, such as the *Independent Monitor* of Tuscaloosa, which if not precisely journalistic, gave to the printed word an impact which even the angriest orthodox newspaper could not achieve. These Klan publications were very influential for a while.

Small wonder that even the emoluments of journalistic dishonesty were not enough to keep the interloper at his desk in those communities where some semblance of law and order and the presence of occupying federal troops fought a discouraged South's avengers and defenders. The end results in such a conflict were not foreseeable in the 1870s. All that the Southerner perceived was the Yankee whom he equated with dishonesty and for his own part, a single goal—the recapture of the political South from the motley combination of Northerners and poor white Southerners whom he looked upon as traitors and a target against which any weapon was fair and a snake to be scotched by any means. Dispassionate and honest journalism died on the vine in much of the South. It would be a long time budding again.

Most of the Southern Democratic newspapers after the war were bombastic organs dominated by men who tried to justify their region and its recent defeat. Caring little for factual reporting, they fulminated against the carpetbagger, the Negro and the Yankee soldier of military Reconstruction. Amazingly enough, few editors were put in jail, the army seeming to have been quite tolerant of their attacks. These editors did succeed in boosting the Southern morale and uniting it in its resistance to Reconstruction, for better or worse.

Dividing the battered region even further were their ideological counterparts, the Republican editors of the occupied South. The latter, who for the most part had come to the South to take her best and leave their worst, edited strict party organs that were established in every Southern community of any size at all. Even before the end of the war, Republican newspapers had been founded in several cities when they fell to Northern troops, or, the political color of an existing newspaper would be changed to suit the occupiers, as happened in Vicksburg and Charleston. If these newspapers had been responsible voices of dissent, history, if not their contemporary South, would have looked upon them with favor. As it happened, only two of the more than 100 Republican newspapers in the South of that time can be considered reputable, unselfish and honest. These were the Savannah *Republican* and the Atlanta *New Era*. The others such as *The Americus Union,* edited by Jay Clarke Swayze in Georgia, and J. E. Bryant's Augusta paper, the *Loyal Georgian,* were vicious, wholly self-seeking journals, that cared not to make the South a truly integrated part of the nation.

Equally as divisive were the Negro Republican journals, which played as big a part as any papers in stirring up racial hatred. One, the New Orleans *Tribune,* was edited by a Negro from Santo Domingo and advocated turning Louisiana into an all-Negro state. Others were the *Weekly Pilot* of Nashville, the *Weekly Planet* of Memphis, and the *Missionary Record.*

None of the editors, except for those getting financial handouts, had an easy time. It was a long hard struggle to rebuild Southern newspapers after the war, the presses and type and other vital equipment being antiquated or difficult to obtain. Moreover, the Southerners were, for the most part, educationally and financially deprived, so that the circulation of the papers took a very slow march upwards.

Despite these handicaps the number of newspapers grew so that while in 1865 there were only 182 weekly Southern newspapers, by 1880 there were ten times as many—1,827.

The leading papers of the period were the Atlanta *Constitution,* the Montgomery *Advertiser,* the Savannah *News,* the Richmond *Dispatch,* the New Orleans *Times-Democrat* and *Picayune,* the Columbia (South Carolina) *State,* the Atlanta *Journal,* the Raleigh *Chronicle,* the Birmingham *News,* the Houston *Chronicle* and the Charlotte *Observer.* Many of these were the product of Yankee editors come South and the quality of the content reflected the education of Northern college men and veteran newspapermen.

From the immediate post-war years on, there had been Southern voices, both within and outside of the journalistic profession, advocating a vote for the freedman on an unrestricted basis. Among these was the untouchable hero of South Carolina, Wade Hampton, who stood against one time foe and one time compatriot to plead the cause of racial justice and an unrestricted ballot. So did James Alcorn, a Mississippi planter, a man who swam against the current and became a Republican, and as a Republican was elected governor of his state. So did Captain Francis Warrington Dawson, the Englishman, whose Charleston *News and Courier* was one of the most moderate voices of the new South. He deeply loved his adopted nation and region, and although he crusaded for the industrial and agricultural reforms that he hoped would put the South on an economic par with the rest of the country, he realized that the most important task ahead was the bringing of the South into the mainstream of American thought. These men spoke with rational voices in a day of irrationality and their usefulness to the South and to the nation has not been properly measured.

The Creole aristocrat, General Pierre Gustave Toutant Beauregard, whose order to fire at Fort Sumter signaled the beginning of the war, cried out in 1873 in perhaps the most remarkable document to emerge from the period of Reconstruction, a manifesto to the people of Louisiana:

I may be mistaken in supposing that a frank and cordial concession of absolute and practical civil, as well as political equality between all citizens, without discrimination on account of race or color, as proposed in this movement, would remove the last barrier which opposes the political co-operation of good men, of whatever color, for the regeneration of the State; but I am earnest in my conviction that I am not mistaken.

Experience seems, at all events, to have demonstrated two propositions quite conclusively, viz: 1st, that without such cooperation the redemption of the State is impracticable; 2d, that such co-operation cannot be secured on any other terms.

Besides, I am profoundly convinced that no sound and lasting system of political philosophy can be constructed under

existing facts in Louisiana, at least, which does not recognize
such equality. Every such system must square itself so as to
consist in all its expressions and implications with the fun-
damental fact of impartial suffrage. When we are asked *why*
we refuse to admit colored people to the enjoyment of public
privileges on a footing of equality with other citizens, it is
not sufficient to say that in so doing we merely exercise a
right for which we are not compelled to give a reason. There
must be some reason or motive at the foundation of all human
conduct. And if at the basis of this course of conduct par-
ticipated in by the mass of the white people of the State,
there does lie a reason so powerful as to defy the provisions
of the constitutions and laws and the decrees of courts, it
certainly concerns the colored man to inquire whether, carried to its logical consequences, it does not threaten other
rights, of which he already has the full enjoyment. Yet I
would ask any one to state why a colored man should not
participate in these public privileges, which would not be a
better reason why he should not serve on a jury, why he
should not hold responsible offices, nay, why he should not
possess the right of suffrage itself!

We are bound to give this great experiment of Republican
self-government, on the basis of impartial suffrage, a fair trial;
and as long as we assume a position antagonistic in principle
to his rights, and thereby drive the colored man into opposition to us, if harm results we must lay the blame upon ourselves, rather than on the system.

The great Southern editors who emerged also realized
the challenges that faced the battered, defeated South and
welcomed the chance to help direct its future. Men like
Henry Watterson of the Louisville *Courier-Journal,*
Henry Grady of the Atlanta *Constitution,* and Adolph
Ochs and John McGowan of the Chattanooga *Times* were
all moderate voices calling for a free system of education,
railroads, industrialization, and, above all, a self-sufficient
South that would bury the worst of the past and look to
the future.

Grady, who was to die when only thirty-nine years old,

first came to national prominence by his magnificent coverage of the Charleston earthquake of 1886. That same year in December he addressed the New England Society of New York at a dinner in that city at Delmonico's. Through this speech describing a New South which he said was growing every hour "not through protest against the old, but because of new conditions, new adjustments, and, if you please, new ideas and aspirations" he became nationally known. More importantly, the Southern press which had, in fact, recognized the same facts, now gave greater editorial support to the drive for change which the forward looking editors knew had to come. The South they sought was a South no longer dependent on farming but industrialized and using its own resources.

Grady's story, "A Pickens County Funeral," humorously points up the new emphasis. He describes therein the funeral of a "one gallus farmer."

They buried him in the midst of a marble quarry; yet a little tombstone they put above him was from Vermont. They buried him in the heart of a pine forest, yet the pine coffin was imported from Cincinnati. They buried him within touch of an iron mine, yet the nails in his coffin and the iron in the shovel that dug his grave were imported from Pittsburgh. They buried him in a New York coat and a Boston pair of shoes . . . breeches from Chicago and shirt from Cincinnati.

Because of their insistence on tackling the problems of Reconstruction with new, and to many Southerners, radical solutions, several of the journalistic crusaders would be financially ruined and forced to discontinue their unwanted advice, so that their readers could retreat into their pre-war mentalities unbothered by the realities of post-war life. In North Carolina, the conservative society of Raleigh was outraged by Walter Hines Page's *State Chronicle* because he dared to tell them that what was past was past and that the South must learn to change with the times. Page, who had remained loyal to the Union, came out for the common man on all issues, without regard to race. He crusaded for social and economic change because he realized the importance to the South of seeing that the poor white and the Negro were a part of it. Eventually, he was forced to sell his financially-unsuccessful newspaper, moving to New York where he was engaged in newspaper and magazine work and in book publishing.

Later in Columbus, Georgia, the forces of bigotry eventually caused the *Enquirer-Sun,* the newspaper owned by Joel Chandler Harris' wife Julia and son Julian, to fold, but not before it had exposed and damaged the Ku Klux Klan and won a Pulitzer Prize for so doing. The *Advertiser* in Montgomery and the *News* and *Age-Herald* in Birmingham were other newspapers that continued to fight racial and economic reaction as pioneers for change well into a century and in a region where change was not welcomed.

The South had been conditioned in the pre-war years to resent criticism by Abolitionists and then by all Northerners. During Reconstruction, as the Southern press worked for the imposition of a white primary, the concept of solidarity of a white South that would brook no question, even by a friend, was reinforced.

A hundred years after the end of the war, the earlier conditioning would bring the old response.

FOUR

Into the Mainstream:
The Southern Press Since 1900

IT IS EASIER TO RECOGNIZE CHANGE ACROSS THE BARRIER OF
time than when walking in the noonday sun of today.
It is easier to mourn the muted voices of the old thun-
derers—the Pulitzers, the Binghams, the Wattersons, the
Gradys, the Ralph McGills—than to seek, and discover,
the new voices that despite the temptation to a modern
newspaper to take care will surely be heard some day.
It is easier to say that newspapers are too alike as likeness
can be than to proclaim the courage of an Atlanta *Journal,* an Atlanta *Constitution,* a St. Louis *Post-Dispatch,*
an *Arkansas Gazette,* and that brave little weekly edited
by a brave woman, Hazel Brannon Smith in Lexington,
Mississippi. The easy way also is to condemn the often
Godforsaken similarities of the daily press rather than
to tell ourselves and the critics of the American press that
the sameness of a great columnist is not evil in itself.
The American newspapers are still unmatched in our
world and among them Southern newspapers can vie
with any in courage, in devotion to ideals, and in standing
up for simple justice against brutal force and man's in-

humanity to man. Throughout the South's history brave
men have died because they cared about such matters.
Some others will die in the years to come. But neither
change nor heroism will die.

For thirty-seven years my newspapers have fought despo-
tism and what we believe to be wrong wherever we perceived their threats. So has many another Southern newspaper, and American newspapers generally. If I may be
personal and perhaps a braggadocio I would like to recall
for you that for four years on our first tiny daily in Hammond, Louisiana, my wife and I took everything that
Huey Long could hurl at us and in the end we were still
alive when he was underground. He couldn't put us out
of business and God knows he tried.

So did an odious man named Theodore G. Bilbo in
Mississippi. So has many another demagogue. And what
we were able to do any newspaper can do and many are
doing it. Ours is still a brave profession.

Let me again be personal. We founded our daily in
Hammond, Louisiana, in April 1932 with less than $500
in capital. A week later we began telling our neighbors
what we thought of Huey P. Long who four years later
paid with his life for his tyranny, a tragic act which even
though we hated him we could not condone; for murder,
whether of the Kennedy brothers for whom I had an
almost-idolatrous affection or of Huey Long himself is not
the American way and should not be civilized man's way
anywhere. We knew what it was to be threatened, to be
boycotted, to be forced to carry a pistol every night when
we went out, and often during the day, to be reviled and
hated by our more-ignorant fellow citizens. But what we
knew best of all was that a man can stand up to his enemies even in depression and against the most violent opposition and still survive. Not only did we survive but the
record my wife and I wrote brought us an invitation and

matching funds to come to the beloved little Mississippi city which is now our home. The incredibly civic-minded citizens of varying political leanings, alike only in the prosperity that had come their way, offered what is still the most fantastic journalistic sponsorship of which I have ever known. They not only matched our money, but they agreed to a hands-off policy and to selling us their stock for what they had put into the paper. Today it is worth more than twenty times what we put in it. Most of these men are dead now but none of them died disliking us, even though we often angered them with editorial expressions which did not echo their own beliefs.

And I know this: that with the backing of these noble citizens our Greenville paper wrought a miracle. Our town had the first Negro policemen in Mississippi. We integrated our public schools and other facilities without a law suit or a single incident of violence. Our polling booths were open to Negroes twenty years ago. We have had three police chiefs in succession who have been completely color-blind. Negroes serve on public bodies in our town, yet all around us are little hell-holes of hate. No one needs to tell my wife and me what a newspaper can do. We proved it for ourselves and for our town. And if I sound as if I'm boasting, it is simply because that's what I am doing.

If what I am saying in these final observations concerning the Southern press and the South today stems from personal biases and opinions, I hope it is understandable. Almost everything I know about journalism derives from my own experiences in a sociologically-retarded area, Louisiana and Mississippi, with occasional forays to larger and more distant and confused places. Of one matter I am certain. I could not have found a more exciting outlet for whatever newspaper talent I may possess than the publishing of three small dailies in Louisiana and Mississippi for more than a third of a century. And in only the Southern states could I have discovered so fully how the traditions of the past remain a part of the present and influence and impinge upon it, especially in the tradition of direct personal action as contrasted with and part of jeremiad editorial expression. It may be that the difficult years of Southern Reconstruction established patterns of activist reaction for Southern editors which persisted in our Southland long after editors elsewhere had retired to the editorial easy chair to let their words alone agitate, infrequently, for a better world.

Let me draw one of many related and relevant anecdotes from a hat I have never worn by choice. I don't even own a hat and let me hasten to add that while such relationships do draw husbands and wives closer together, I do not recommend shotgun law even though I think it was justified in this case and since we were temporarily law officers of sorts, we were within our rights.

At a time when Huey Long ran roughshod over civil and human rights in Louisiana and condemnatory front-page editorials in my *Daily Courier* at Hammond were almost daily occurrences, a group of protesters in the Sixth Congressional District sought successfully, if not pacifically, to halt wrongs and dictatorial usurpation of the political processes. One part of the issue was an attempt by the Long forces to stage a special election without benefit of the usual party primary which should have preceded it. An anti-Long judge ruled the Long-called election to be illegal. The judge swore in a number of rather tough deputies with instructions to halt the proposed balloting and sent these deputies out the night before the fraudulent election with the comment that it was a poor judge who couldn't enforce his own rulings. We stopped that election. And my share was not confined to editorial support. One of my personal weapons was a beautiful Mexican sawed-off shotgun. But I appeared less of a hero than I had hoped because as a group of deputies walked down our front steps, I heard behind me a rather timorous voice. It was my wife. She said, "Dear, you've forgotten your shotgun."

Thanks to the shotgun and other firearms, we prevented that election and gave Long his only political defeat in all the years of his power.

But this story has not so much to do with a Mexican shotgun as with the kind of political society in which we were forced to live in those days and the fact that an editor like his predecessors of the post-Civil War period accepted with alacrity the role of posseman. It really wasn't fun. There is no fun in hate and what was spawned in the gleaming marble hall of the Louisiana capitol was the bloody aftermath of hatred. A quiet, non-political man killed a dictator because of an unforgivable insult to his wife and her family.

In the intervening years I have heard few, if any, stories of editors participating in like manner in political situations. Perhaps the need has not existed. But the fact remains that as late as the 1930s some of the Louisiana editors saw the backing up of editorials with action as an editorial duty. In that fact one can discern evidence of the emotionalism that for so long served to set Southern journalism apart from that of the rest of the nation.

The Southern press, if I may be permitted to speak in generalities, has been the pugnacious, more easily aroused, and less rational member of the family. This has been true almost from the beginning. It was certainly true after the slavery controversy, the War Between the States and Reconstruction became the all absorbing issues. Moreover, the perpetuation of the old, once deadly tradition of highly personal and vengeful newspaper publishing has not helped us as a nation or a region. To realize this truth

we have only to ponder what might have been the outcome of civil, regional conflict, short of war, had the South
enjoyed the journalistic flowering that so considerably
characterized the Eastern press in the generation before
the outbreak of intersectional strife. What if we could
have produced our Greeleys, our Bennetts, our Danas, and
our Pulitzers and turned over to them newspapers fit for
their talents. How much more would we have known
about our fellow Americans and ourselves had we had
someone or recruited during these years of impending
tragedy someone who saw the issue and the South's terrible mistakes with their clarity. How much more secure
would our nation have become had the editor scorned the
Bowie knife and the shotgun and the pistol as weapons
to prove how right he was. Fewer heroes, yes. Fewer absolute triumphs, yes again. Few fallen men, yes.

I do not want to pause overlong with the past. The
Southern press as a spiritual and political force perpetu-
ating a world that was dead has lasted too long. But what
can come to replace it? What is needed now is to ask
ourselves where and what is the Southern newspaper today, and where it is going and why. I am all the more
uneasy in my answers because I know they are true.

Obviously, there is no such single entity as the Southern
newspaper. The South has its metropolitan Goliaths as
does the North in such newspapers as the New Orleans
Times-Picayune, the Miami *Herald,* the Atlanta *Constitution,* the Atlanta *Journal,* the Nashville *Tennessean*
and *Banner,* the Birmingham *Age-Herald,* the Louisville
Courier-Journal, the Charlotte *News and Observer,* the
newspapers of Houston and Dallas, the Memphis *Commercial Appeal* and others less large and wealthy if none-
theless professionally powerful.

Today, after nearly a century of change, the Southern
metropolitan newspaper is greatly unlike its predecessors,

for the daily newspaper almost everywhere now speaks with the voice of big business. The change is nearly absolute. Almost no matter where the American newspaper is published today, fewer independent dailies, either in thought or expression or personality, remain in our land. They are assembly-line productions, most of them, as like as peas in a pod. And if the editors don't like it this way, the publishers seemingly do. Probably the most difficult problem of the Southern newspaper today, shared by papers throughout the nation, is how to survive as an independent unit in a time of chain ownership and big business. How can the Southern press enter the mainstream of American journalism without sacrificing regional loyalties and needs? It is almost a cliché today to lament the sameness of the Southern and national press, and we mourn the vanished editor who speaks for himself and tells those of his readers who don't like what he has to say to go to hell. How can the small publisher himself survive? How can he meet the challenge of television and radio without seeking monopolies in these allied fields? How can he be judicious and temperate at a time when an ancient regional fever of mistrust and bitterness again possesses us?

Today the Southern press more than ever falls into categories that have no relation to size. Some of them are good newspapers yet, some of them are incredibly poor, only a few are published in competitive newspaper communities. These monopolistic papers could stand up as their predecessors once stood up to material odds. The difference today is the overwhelming importance of the dollar.

Most of the questions I have posed have answers. One of them will be born of technological revolution which will make it far less expensive to print a newspaper. Another will mirror the rootlessness of a nation where people will no longer react as did their fathers. Still another will portray the changed occupations of a region becoming increasingly industrial. And would it be too much to suggest that some of the questions have a spiritual answer?

For there is one Southern distinction that yet endures. It is a spiritual one and it may well be that when the definitive history of the Southern press is written, the persistence with which the South and the Southern press have clung to the simpler spiritual values may be the abiding identification. This I believe from my heart. Men still defend their convictions more ardently in the South than elsewhere, in the tradition of the frontier. Some even see the shadow of God above the shadow of the pen poised angrily above a sheet of foolscap. For this the South and the nation can thank that God.

If one word could be selected to recur as a common denominator of American culture in our parlous times, that word would be sameness, the protesting aberrations of hippiedom to the contrary. Drive down any main street of any community large enough to boast a Woolworth's store and sameness will hit you between the eyes with a jarring impact which dulls the senses rather than bruises the body. One after another the disciples of sameness have placed their stamp through the J. C. Penney Companies, the Sears Roebuck stores, the Rexall drug stores, the Kroger supermarkets, the branch banks, the filling stations, the Dairy Queens, the assortment of chain cheapjack stores.

This is not to say that the result is all bad or even mostly bad. Mass production and mass distribution are providing the American people with color and a variety of luxuries—most of which we could do without—along with sameness, with limits often in bad taste but nevertheless of infinite variety. The American wife can find a greater selection in dresses and shoes and children's clothing and the American husband in slacks and shirts at prices that, taking inflation into due account, still make us at reasonable relative cost the warmest or the coolest and the best-dressed people anywhere to be found.

And this is happening in a South which once subsisted at a near-starvation level, as well as in the nation as a whole.

Let the length of a dress or the color of a suit be pre-scribed in some distant place, whether in Paris or New York or Los Angeles, and everyone falls into line. To me one of the most amusing as well as one of the most pa-thetic aspects of women's ready-to-wear clothing is the established and accepted custom of garment manufac-turers known as "knocking down." Because of this it is impossible for an exclusive model to remain exclusive very long. Let a Dior or a Saint-Laurent creation appear today and tomorrow the garment cutters of New York's Seventh Avenue will be engaged in a denigration which ends up with a reasonable facsimile of a $1,000 original going on the market for $50 and down. And they can be bought in 500 Southern towns by rich women, poor women, black women, and white women who read about the cost of the creation in the local paper. But what does this spell? Not so much style as sameness. For the Colonel's Lady and Judy O'Grady thereby become sisters over the skin.

It is valid now to extend the symptoms and the fact of sameness to all fields of communications. Select at random a half-dozen newspapers of comparable circulation with-out regard to the regions in which they are published. If there is a sameness to styles and store fronts and merchan-dise in general, consider the most dangerous of American conformities, that of the press.

Turn first, as probably a majority of American news-paper readers do, to the comic page. Within the confines of space, the comic strips are as like as like. You have your choice of Mary Worth, Rex Morgan, Judge Parker, or

Brenda Starr—the soap operas in cartoon form. Or, you can choose from Blondie, Maggie and Jiggs, Snuffy Smith, and the like. It won't matter which you prefer to read, as they are almost all endless repeats of the same basic jokes.

In the last twenty-five years only two real innovations in comic strips have been made. One, which appeared in the short-lived experimental daily, *P.M.,* a paper which lost ten million dollars for Marshall Field while trying to be different, concerned an angelic chap named Barnaby. He was so far ahead of most of his readers that he didn't last long. The other innovation, Charles Schulz's Peanuts, is so good that it has spawned several books and a current theatre hit called *You're a Good Man, Charlie Brown.* A few others have differed: among them are B. C., Pogo, and Lil Abner, the latter two having a zanily Southern flavor.

But newspapers, contrary to what some may believe, are not made up of comic strips alone, nor are they intended primarily to be purveyors of such strips. So let's look at the other sections. On the woman's page of each of these papers you can have your choice of the warring sisters, Ann Landers or Dear Abby. They're good. I happen to think that Ann is better. But it is not a good thing to have to make a choice between them, even with "Hints from Heloise" thrown in. Nor is it especially pleasing to the journalistic senses for the woman's page accounts of luncheons and weddings and debutante parties to read with such stereotyped sameness that it requires but the change of a few names and the description of the decor to make the stories interchangeable.

We seem to be working from back to front. Let's look now at the sports pages of our selected papers. Among sports writers can be found more originality and enthusiasm than is discernable on most other pages save for the exceptional editorial page. The sports editors like to go to war with each other. They are positive in their art of thinking and they take good care of the home town boys on the gridiron and diamond and court. But go through these six newspapers and select sports vocabularies. They are more often identical than not, at least as far as the mainstream of sports comment is concerned. It takes a Babe Ruth, a Babe Didrikson, or a Cassius Clay to evoke flammably original prose.

Let us move further toward the front page, skipping over those pages which print the secondary general news. We survey now the editorial page. The editorials of our newspapers vary according to whether they are Republican, Democratic, Republican with a splash of liberalism, Democratic with a splash of conservatism, conservative conservative, or liberal liberal, or racially motivated. Whatever their point of view, most of the editorials on these pages are deadly dull and carefully tailored to the demands of the business office. If this seems too harsh a comment, read the editorial columns for yourself. What newspapers, North and South, need most of all is editors and reporters who can write or more importantly who can think. And this is more true in the South than elsewhere because the Southern journalist with talent who heads North can usually make enough there to buy a steak for himself and his wife and the kiddies rather than just hamburger. It has been a tragedy of our democracy that the three greatest spiritual outlets for the mind of man are the least rewarded. They are the press, the teaching profession, and the ministry. The worst manifestation of the editorial column today is that it reflects something which many Americans overlook, namely enervating, mentally-debilitating sameness which stems from absentee and chain ownership and the demands of the business office that there be no journalistic liberties except those having to do with the dollar. The South has been the last resister to the cult of sameness, but we are fast catching up.

Once the Southern newspapers did not fit this pattern. The Southern press could count more individualists, however emotional their approach to the stormy issues of the day, than could newspapers in any other section of the country once they took personal issue which at least showed fiery conviction. Once they refused to wear the other man's collar. Once the dollar was not paramount.

It is 100 years now since the citizens of a beleaguered Vicksburg read brief little newspapers that were printed on wallpaper. It is more than seventy-five years since a resurgent South dreamed of and in considerable part accomplished a journalistic revolution in the wake of a terrible holocaust, a revolution which involved editorship and ownership and individualism in the use of the printed word and a change of economic direction that made the Gradys and Wattersons the spokesmen for a new and hopeful South whose realization is only now being consummated. Only a general unity of racial attitude persisted and even this was not universal.

The sameness which haunts American culture in general today is omnipresent among its newspapers. As has been said herein, this sameness has merit but it also does our mid-twentieth century society a great harm. We are too much alike from our main streets to our newspaper composing rooms. And while this may make the publishers of region and nation more secure and wealthier, we also suffer harm because of uniformity. Today there is little difference between daily newspapers and weekly newspapers anywhere in our land. Our news services reflect a shrinking society but they do not speak with the dissimilar, thundering voice of a Greeley of New York or a Rhett of South Carolina. No people in the South or the nation ever printed the full-page food advertisements that we scan so casually in every community, small and large, across the nation. The world is not only too much with us it is too much of the same world. And this is not good. I have no wish to moralize. I do wish that I published an American newspaper in some other today and under other circumstances. And so does every newspaper editor who takes pride in individualism and who likes a fight. I don't know what to do about it. I do know that I don't like the way things are today. Maybe change will come but I doubt it. Today if we say that newspaper X is Republican and newspaper Y is Democratic, we speak of the same coin. In the past thirty years my *Delta Democrat-Times* has supported Republican candidates for the presidency three times and Democrats for the rest of the time.

Reading what we have written on political matters over the years I see little difference today in what I have said in behalf of a Wilkie or a Roosevelt. Most of the political figures are basically decent men but they do not differ greatly from each other nor do the causes they espouse. And I know it is not good to walk with sameness throughout one's life, especially as a newspaper publisher. Perhaps this is a sour note. I still take pride in the American press even while I sorrow for its spiritual degeneration. I am proud of the brave editors of a century ago when their bravery was respected by an enemy more honorable than those who seek today to destroy us in our land.

It is pleasant to make money in a society so devoted to that talent but in all earnestness I can say as a Southerner that I would rather be poor and challenging than a well-to-do conformist, for conformity is the curse of our nation and our region. Was George Washington a conformist? Was Thomas Jefferson a conformist? Was a Monroe or a Madison a conformist? Was Andrew Jackson a conformist? Was Franklin Delano Roosevelt a conformist? God help our country if they had been. They were first of all tough Americans.

Some final observations must be made, for they concern

the most revolutionary period in the history of Southern journalism.

The Supreme Court desegregation decision of 1954, and the court decisions, administrative orders, and congressional acts which followed, presented the Southern press with its greatest opportunity for leadership in this century. Most of the press, no less than most of the politicians, responded miserably.

This is a harsh assessment, which should be and will be tempered with the obvious exceptions. But at a time when editors and publishers should have been responsive to the demands of the Constitution and conscience, they harkened far more closely to the imperatives of a society —in this case white—which saw itself again engaged in civil war, a war in which virtually no holds have been barred and whose result could only be total victory or total defeat. For many editors and publishers the response was honest: they shared the values of the land they inhabited and felt it their duty to reflect them. Too many others surrendered to simple and not so simple expediency: to do other than to follow the politicians and the organized segregationists was to court economic retaliation. The First Amendment proved in too many cases to mean far less than the balance sheet.

For a period of a few weeks or months following the 1954 decision, it seemed that the press, like the region, might be prepared to accommodate itself to some measure of desegregation. Such newspaper editors as Grover Hall of the Montgomery *Advertiser* and James J. Kilpatrick of the Richmond *News Leader* sounded almost moderate. But this was a false start for both men, and for a majority of the newspapers of the middle and deep South. Soon enough the transplanted Oklahoman, Kilpatrick, was dusting off interposition as the South's legitimate answer to court-ordered desegregation, and Hall, whose father had been an early foe of the Ku Klux Klan and a Pulitzer Prize winner, changed position entirely to embrace the citizens councils as respectable repositories of defiance.

Perhaps this should not have been unexpected. The Southern press is, for the most part, embedded in small towns and smallish cities. It is not unusual for the publishers of any paper, North or South, to reflect the status quo; it is far more difficult personally for any non-conformist who is not lucky enough to live in a big city, and big cities are the exception in the South.

In short, it took something more than intellectual integrity for the Southern dissenter who was also a journalist to lift his voice. He also needed courage, physical as well as moral, because there was no ivory tower retreat from outside pressures. These pressures abounded and included his biggest advertisers and his meanest foemen, prepared to shoot from ambush.

But there were Southern newspapermen who possessed the necessary qualities and met the test. In Virginia, whose newspapers generally fell into line behind massive resistance, the Norfolk *Virginian-Pilot* (whose Lenoir Chambers won the Pulitzer Prize for editorial writing in 1960) came out early in favor of the Supreme Court decision and never wavered. If Kilpatrick's *News Leader* brayed that "this tyranny must be resisted, step by step and inch by inch," the *Virginian-Pilot* hailed the decision as a "superb appeal to the wisdom, intelligence and leadership of the Southern states." It was finally the *News Leader*, not the *Virginian-Pilot*, which found it necessary to reverse editorial course in the face of reality in the 1960s.

The miserable Jackson *Daily News*, which with its sister publication the Jackson *Clarion-Ledger* has been unequalled to this day in journalistic bigotry, led the general press attack in Mississippi against any accommodation with desegregation. "You Are For Us Or Against Us," its late editor Fred Sullens proclaimed, and most Mississippi newspapers agreed. But not all. Perhaps the most courageous of Mississippi editors was and is Hazel Brannon Smith of Lexington, a small and improbable spot for heroism. But heroic is hardly a strong enough word for what this indomitable believer in the rights of all men did. In the face of boycott, personal harassment, bombings, cross burnings, and the creation of a rival weekly newspaper by the citizens council leadership of her county, she continued to proclaim clearly, emphatically, and persistently her deep-felt conviction that racist inhumanity is intolerable. Hazel Smith won a Pulitzer Prize for her stand, as well as the undying hatred of every racist in Mississippi, but more importantly she proved that honesty could not be silenced if it would not be silenced.

There were others in Mississippi, although only a handful when measured against the total number of newspapers in the state. Ira Harkey in Pascagoula, Oliver Emmerich in McComb, Hal DeCell in Rolling Fork, and George McClain in Tupelo, and my own newspaper all held to the belief that decency, moderation, and accommodation should be the region's response to inevitable change. All but Harkey are still in Mississippi and still writing what they believe. And, may I add here, pridefully, that my eldest son, Hodding Carter III, chose to return to Mississippi after his Princeton graduation and a tour in the Marines to serve ably his native state and South as editor of my *Delta Democrat-Times*.

Gone, but certainly not forgotten, is P. D. East, whose little *Petal Paper* was the gadfly of segregationist insanity and a weekly boost to the flagging spirits of the moderate-liberal underground of the state's closed society. It was probably an impossible task for the editor of a newspaper whose circulation never topped 2,500, but East went at his opponents as though they were the minority and he the majority—until they proved he was wrong. His was probably the strangest newspaper ever published in the South, and actually it was not a newspaper but a journal dedicated to the expression of one lonely man's opinions. Vastly different but with the same objective was Harry Golden, the humorist and satirist, who published in Charlotte, North Carolina, the *Carolina Israelite*, until he, like East, folded his tent.

Two newspapers and three newspapermen stood out as beacons of hope for all those in the region who felt that desegregation was morally and politically right, and massive resistance a brutal charade which could have no effect except to produce frustration, violence, and economic stagnation. One was the late Ralph McGill of the Atlanta *Constitution*, who fought the good fight in Georgia for decades until his death on February 3, 1969. For him there was no possible compromise with the demands of law and justice on the one hand or with bigotry on the other. The former he proclaimed as his own credo, the latter he fought at every turn. If Ralph McGill did not gain his region's love, he gained its respect, and he had the satisfaction of seeing Atlanta move ahead in comparative racial peace while the citadels of violent resistance came to violent crossroads.

A city which did not deserve to be there and would not have been but for the political ambitions of one man was Little Rock. In a few short days in 1957 the Arkansas capital became synonymous with segregationist fury, thanks to the machinations of Governor Orval Faubus. But it also became synonymous with journalistic courage, thanks to Harry Ashmore, editor of the *Arkansas Gazette*, and its owner, J. N. Heiskel. As Heiskel put it, "there comes a time when a newspaperman has to decide whether

to follow his conscience or material considerations." Heiskel, probably the most courageous of the Deep South's
newspapermen, laid everything he had on the line and
Ashmore was his public voice. Never before or since has a
newspaper and its editor won a Pulitzer Prize simulta-
neously. As a member at the time of the Pulitzer Advisory
Board which selects the prize winners in all categories I
think it is proper to record that the board's decision was
unanimous in both categories. The *Gazette* lost many battles, including an almost disastrous toll in circulation can-
cellations and advertising, but it has been steadily winning
the war for itself and Arkansas.

The *Gazette* is not alone in Arkansas. The Pine Bluff
Commercial is a calm voice of sanity in one part of the
state while Tom Dearmore's *Baxter Bulletin* in Mountain
Home, Arkansas, is another.

And across the South similar voices were heard in the
1950s and are heard even more vigorously in the 1960s.
North Carolina, from Jonathan Daniels' *News and Observer* to Pete McKnight's *Charlotte Observer,* to mention
only two, has been singularly fortunate in the quality of
its newspapers and their editorial courage. The Louisville
Courier Journal led the fight for school desegregation in
the mid-1950s and has not rested on its laurels since then.
In Gainesville, Georgia, Sylvan Meyer's *Times* represents
everything which small-town journalism should mean and
too rarely does: editorial integrity and full community
coverage. Buford Boone, with his Tuscaloosa *News,*
showed the way for his more timorous brethren in Ala-
bama journalism in 1956 and continues to do so.

This does not complete the list, but it does illustrate a
sad fact about Southern journalism. For every Hazel Brannon Smith or Sylvan Meyer or Buford Boone, there were
a dozen editors or publishers who took the easiest or most-
popular way out. Some came belatedly to the realization

that freedom of the press also carried with it responsibilities, and that leadership was first among them, but many even today have not done so.

Even for some of the best, good, hard depth reporting was more honored as a concept than a reality. The editorial thunder could roll, but the reader too often simply was not informed about much more than the surface froth of the deep wave of change which was, and is, engulfing our region. Those newspapers which did report events relating to the integration struggle (and there were a shamefully-large number which would not even do this) rarely went deeper than the events themselves. That there was agitation for a given change—such as better schools or jobs or housing— was duly reported. Why the agitation existed was rarely explored and what other conditions might require attention were not exposed. The prevalence of malnutrition among literally millions of Southerners came as a shock. The long-lasting effects of the transition from hand labor to mechanization on the farms and the exodus which ensued was virtually ignored. The Southern press was static in its news beats. It is a *mea culpa* from which few Southern newspapers can be exempted.

And yet the changes were being reported by Southerners. The catch was that they did not work for Southern newspapers. John Popham and then Claude Sitton of the New York *Times,* based in Atlanta, traveled through the length and breadth of the South and delved deeply in their reports into the issues behind the issues. Jack Nelson, a white Mississippian who once wrote for the Atlanta *Constitution,* today gives the readers of the Los Angeles *Times* and the *Times-Washington Post* news service a far better perspective on the South than the readers of the average Southern newspaper could hope to obtain. Walter Rugaber, Roy Reed, and John Herberts of the New York *Times,* Southerners all, did the same, as does Joe Cummings of *Newsweek's* Atlanta bureau. They did the job the wire services only belatedly decided they could and should do and which many Southern newspapers have yet to do.

Southern television journalism for most of the period was either duly meshed into service for the segregationist cause, like WLBT-TV of Jackson during the 1950s and early 1960s, or contented itself with a castrated capsulation of the news designed to offend as few whites as possible and to ignore the Negro community at all costs. But again there were exceptions, with WDSU-TV of New Orleans the most outstanding. In a city whose newspapers for most of the pre-1954 period were either stand-pat or silent, WDSU editorialized in favor of change and covered the news in comprehensive fashion. It was and is what television journalism should be and usually isn't.

The black press has not been a significant factor in the region except in isolated areas. In some places, and Jackson is one, Negro newspapers became the captives of the white power structure and the delight of the segregationists who used reprints of their editorials to buttress the arguments for the status quo. In other cities, such as Atlanta, they sometimes provided articulate expression of the Negro minority's viewpoint. And one newspaper, the *Southern Courier,* a worthwhile experiment which died while still in its infancy, provided a tantalizing glimpse of how much goes unreported beneath the surface of every Southern town's black population. The glimpse, unfortunately, has not been enough to open the eyes of most deep Southern editors to the legitimate demands of the black community for full and honest coverage.

No appraisal of the Southern press during the post-1954 period would be complete without mentioning the work of the Southern Education Reporting Service during the 1950s and 1960s. It was an invaluable enterprise which sought to compile and present an objective monthly report of what was happening on the school desegregation scene across the South. Its objectivity was never questioned and if its state-by-state surveys were not as complete as they might have been, this was more a reflection of the failure of the press of each state to cover the story fully than of any lack of desire on Southern Education Reporting Service's part.

Perhaps a statement of faith is not needed here. In choosing to make one I realize that my own is not regional and that fellow newspapermen everywhere share my beliefs and motivations. But I am a Southerner by ancestry, by birth, by upbringing, by residence and by choice. As a Southerner I believe that the South needs now as it needed more than a century ago a special dedication because of special problems which have so long plagued us—problems, it should be said, that are being discovered not to be regional at all. So I set down here a credo which has been a guide to some of my predecessors and contemporaries and disregarded by some others. I would not be honest if I did not state my conviction that there remain too many of the latter and too few of the former.

I do believe that mine is a peculiarly-dedicated profession just as are the ministry and teaching. We have objectives which of themselves have nothing to do with the making of money or friends. Newspaper editing is a challenge to pursue unending goals, all of which represent the same challenge. Briefly stated the goals are these:

> to keep men informed,
> to make men think,
> to make men ashamed,
> and to keep men free.

I am a Southerner, I repeat, and I speak with prejudice. I love the land of my ancestors. I am cognizant of the fact that we were the only nation within a nation and that we were destroyed by musket and bayonet and that we came back. Some of the trappings may be vengeful, but the South has not been a land of long vengeance. We belong.

SELECTIVE BIBLIOGRAPHY

Acheson, Sam. *35,000 Days in Texas: A History of the Dallas News and Its Forebears.* New York: Macmillan Co., 1938.

Ambler, C. H. *Thomas Ritchie: A Study in Virginia Politics.* Richmond: Bell Book & Stationery Co., 1913.

Anderson, John Q. *With the Bark On: Popular Humor of the Old South.* Nashville: Vanderbilt University Press, 1967.

Ball, W. W. *The State that Forgot: South Carolina's Surrender to Democracy.* Indianapolis: Bobbs-Merrill Co., 1932.

Bell, E. L. *The Augusta Chronicle: Indomitable Voice of Dixie.* Athens: University of Georgia Press, 1960.

Brantley, Rabun Lee. *Georgia Journalism of the Civil War Period.* Nashville: George Peabody College for Teachers, 1929.

Carter, Hodding. *Lower Mississippi.* New York: Farrar & Rinehart, Inc., 1942.

Cash, Wilbur J. *The Mind of the South.* New York: A. A. Knopf, 1941.

Clark, Thomas D. *The Rural Press and the New South.* Baton Rouge: Louisiana State University Press, 1948.

_____. *The Southern Country Editor.* Indianapolis: Bobbs-Merrill Co., 1948.

Cohen, Hennig, and William B. Dillingham, editors. *Humor of the Old Southwest.* Boston: Houghton Mifflin Company, 1964.

Copeland, Fayette. *Kendall of the Picayune.* Norman: University of Oklahoma Press, 1943.

Coulter, E. Merton. *William G. Brownlow, Fighting Parson of the Southern Highlands.* Chapel Hill: University of North Carolina Press, 1937.

_____. *The Confederate States of America, 1861-1865.* Baton Rouge: Louisiana State University Press, 1950.

_____. *The South During Reconstruction, 1865-1877.* Baton Rouge: Louisiana State University Press, 1947.

Dabney, Thomas E. *One Hundred Great Years: The Story of the Times-Picayune from Its Founding to 1940.* Baton Rouge: Louisiana State University Press, 1944.

Daniels, Josephus. *Tar Heel Editor.* Chapel Hill: University of North Carolina Press, 1939.

Duchein, Annette Ogden. "The Anglo-Saxon Press of New Orleans, 1835-1861." Unpublished Master's Thesis, Louisiana State University, Baton Rouge, 1933.

Eaton, Clement. *A History of the Old South.* New York: Macmillan, 1949.

——————————. *The Freedom of Thought Struggle in the Old South.* New York: Macmillan, 1964.

——————————. *The Growth of Southern Civilization: 1790-1860.* New York: Harper, 1961.

——————————. *A History of the Southern Confederacy.* New York: Macmillan, 1954.

Fisher, Paul L. and Ralph L. Lowenstein, eds. *Race and the News Media.* New York: Praeger, 1967.

Hendrick, Burton J. *The Training of an American: The Early Life and Letters of Walter Hines Page.* Boston: Houghton Mifflin Co., 1928.

Henry, R. H. *Editors I Have Known Since the Civil War.* Jackson, Miss.: R. H. Henry, 1922.

Krock, Arthur. *Editorials of Henry Watterson,* Louisville Courier-Journal Company, 1923.

Lee, James Melvin. *History of American Journalism.* Boston: Houghton Mifflin Co., 1923.

Luxon, Norval Neil. *Nile's Weekly Register.* Baton Rouge: Louisiana State University Press, 1947.

Meine, Franklin J. *Tall Tales of the Southwest.* New York: A. A. Knopf, 1930.

Mott, Frank Luther. *American Journalism: A History, 1690-1960.* 3rd ed. New York: Macmillan, 1962.

Nixon, R. B. *Henry W. Grady.* New York: A. A. Knopf, 1943.

Rosewater, Victor. *History of Cooperative News Gathering in the United States.* New York: Appleton Co., 1930.

Simkins, Francis Butler. *A History of the South.* New York: A. A. Knopf, 1963.

Wall, Joseph F. *Henry Watterson, Reconstructed Rebel.* New York: Oxford University Press, 1956.

Index